LIFE BEGINS AT FIFTY-SOMETHING

*A*n essential guide
to planning for change

MORNA STURROCK

Angus&Robertson
An imprint of HarperCollins*Publishers*

Angus & Robertson
An imprint of HarperCollins*Publishers*, Australia

First published in Australia in 1996
by HarperCollins*Publishers* Pty Limited
ACN 009 913 517
A member of the HarperCollins*Publishers* (Australia) Pty Limited Group

Copyright © Morna Sturrock 1996

This book is copyright.
Apart from any fair dealing for the purposes of private study,
research, criticism or review, as permitted under the Copyright Act,
no part may be reproduced by any process without written
permission. Inquiries should be addressed to the publishers.

HarperCollins*Publishers*
25 Ryde Road, Pymble, Sydney NSW 2073, Australia
31 View Road, Glenfield, Auckland 10, New Zealand
77–85 Fulham Palace Road, London W6 8JB, United Kingdom
Hazelton Lanes, 55 Avenue Road, Suite 2900, Toronto, Ontario, M5R 3L2
and 1995 Markham Road, Scarborough, Ontario M1B 5M8, Canada
10 East 53rd Street, New York NY 10032, USA

The National Library of Australia Cataloguing-in-Publication data:

Sturrock, Morna.
  Life begins at fifty-something : an essential guide to
  planning for change.
  ISBN 0 207 18838 6.
  1. Middle aged persons – Life skills guides. I. Title.
305.244

Designed by Rose Franzoni
Cover design by Rose Franzoni
Cover image by Vladimir Kanigher
Typeset in Australia by Emtype Desktop Publishing
Printed in Australia by Griffin Paperbacks

9 8 7 6 5 4 3 2 1
99 98 97 96

Every effort has been made to ensure that this book is free from error or omissions.
However, the author and publisher shall not accept responsibility for injury, loss or damage
occasioned to any person acting or refraining from action as a result of material in this book
whether or not such injury, loss or damage is in any way due to any negligent act or
omission, breach of duty or default on the part of the author or publisher or their agents.

Our thanks go to those who have given us permission to reproduce copyright material in
this book. Particular sources of print material are acknowledged in the text. Every effort has
been made to contact the copyright holders of print material, and the publisher welcomes
communication from any copyright holder from whom permission was inadvertently not
gained.

Contents

Acknowledgments	**viii**
Introduction	**ix**
1 Early planning	**1**
Take time to dream	2
Financial planning	3
Pointers for successful retirement	6
Age discrimination unlawful	7
2 Humanising the workplace	**11**
Work and families	12
Counselling for change	12
Outplacement	14
Strategies for successful people	15
3 Transition – to what?	**18**
Trying alternative roles	20
Acknowledge the crisis and act	22
Bad learning about life	24
The adolescent Australian male	26
Dry rot in the tree of life	27
The Darwin cyclone experience	29

4 Leisure and recreation – spending time or using time? — 31
    Leisure happens within us — 32
    Some likely objectives — 34
    Leisure as a challenge — 38
    Arts and crafts – a rich repertoire — 40
    Performing arts — 41
    Visual arts — 42
    Busy hands – quiet mind — 43

5 Contributing to a thinking society — 47
    The value of the volunteer — 47
    'Turning thinking into a hobby' — 52
    Learning: a lifelong process — 53
    Dynamic seventy-year-olds – and over — 54
    College for Seniors — 55
    Open Learning Australia — 56
    University of the Third Age — 57
    Short courses for the over-fifties — 60
    Adult Learners Week — 61
    Adult learning centres in rural Australia — 62

6 Are you keeping well? — 65
    Nutrition — 66
    Weight control — 68
    Calcium intake — 69
    Let's take heart — 71
    'Active at any age' — 72
    Keeping up appearances — 76
    Caring for the carers — 78
    Getting on top of it — 81
    A good night's sleep — 84
    Therapeutic massage — 85
    Substance abuse — 86
    Don't worry – it may never happen — 89

7	**Health and gender difference**	**97**
	Men's health	98
	Women's health	104
8	**Beating the statistics**	**113**
	Diet and cancer	114
	Colorectal cancer	115
	Skin cancers	116
	Cancer of the breast	117
	Cancer of the cervix	120
	Prostate cancer	121
	Arthritis – the neglected field	122
	Diabetes	128
9	**Planning the future down on the farm**	**131**
	Transferring the family farm	132
	Legal issues for farm women	136
	The 'silly old bugger syndrome'	138
	Networks for women across rural Australia	143
10	**Repartnering in the nineties**	**152**
	The second time around – or even the first	152
	The stepfamily	156
	To partner or not to partner	159
	The need for intimacy	162
	Disinterest in sex	163
	The right to sexual fulfilment	165
	Menopause	166
11	**Money matters – but how much?**	**169**
	Financial advice	169
	Budgeting in retirement	171
	Superannuation	175
	After retirement	179
	Housing matters	180
	Leave a will, or leave a mess	183

12 Crossing the boundary of loss and grief 189
  The value of funeral rites 190
  Bereavement and health 191
  The wisdom of planning a funeral 192
  Grief counselling 195
  Unique funeral link 199

13 Tomorrow is opportunity waiting 201
  A deliciously exciting age 201
  A mind stretched in search of self 202
  The role of peacemaker 203

Useful resources 205

'I shall soon be fifty. It is high time I got to know myself.'

Stendhal, Rome 1833

Acknowledgments

There are many people to thank for their assistance and expertise in the preparation of this book.

First there is the Life Planning Foundation of Australia, formerly the Early Planning for Retirement Association, whose philosophy about living a full and creative life in one's later years accords so happily with my own.

Robin Freeman, Health and Personal Development Publisher at HarperCollins, had the imagination to invite me to write the book, and with Helen Pace has been supportive throughout the project.

Every individual and every organisation named in the text has been an important resource, for without them the writing would have been impossible. I thank them all.

This book is dedicated to my fairy god-daughter Meredith Fuller, who is still a long way from fifty-something. She continues to have faith in me.

Introduction

If you have turned forty, this book is for you. The sooner you take time to think about the next half of your life, the fuller and more satisfying it will be. Planning can be both a pleasure and a challenge, and the great advantage is that you can change your mind, often! It's not necessarily the immediate outcome of your planning that matters, it's the *process* of thinking ahead, for that in itself can become a way of life.

Life holds few certainties for the forty-somethings, let alone the fifty-somethings. Yet statistics abound. At fifty years, women may now expect to live at least until eighty-one, men until seventy-six, and our life expectancy keeps on rising. In 1964, nearly twenty-four per cent of men aged sixty-five and over were still working; by 1987, the number had shrunk to eight per cent, and the decline was similar for women. It is this older age group that has the greatest opportunity to be liberated, for about ninety-five per cent of them are not going to show any signs of senility; rather, with a positive outlook they will be more than ever ready for growth and development.

What will they do with themselves? They have by no means completed the long-distance race we call life. How will they live happily and healthily? Their best chance is to think ahead and plan, because those of us who have done so are proving life really can be lived to its fullest in that long last half. Our age must not be defined simply as a deterioration from youth.

A major survey commissioned by the Federal Government in 1994, on 'Attitudes to Ageing and Well-being into the Next Century', sought the views of more than 2000 Australians aged 40–55, and 55–75. The findings made it possible for the report to be titled 'An Optimistic Future'. Many may have been predictable, but the key findings are worth reporting here:

- One in three people surveyed look forward to the future 'because it offers new challenges and new things to do'.
- Ninety per cent of the people surveyed believed they were in good, very good or excellent health.
- Many older people believe that growing older gives them the freedom to do what they want to do, but this is offset by concern over physical decline.
- The main health worries for those over fifty-five are obesity, arthritis, worry, lack of exercise, lethargy, frustration, loneliness and lack of motivation.
- Many older Australians believe they have something to offer the community and have an important role to play within the community and within the family.
- Half the people surveyed believe that, as they grow older, they are treated with more respect by other members of the community.
- Three-quarters agreed there should be more opportunities for older people to develop new skills and to adapt to changing technology.
- Most people want to remain living independently in their own homes for as long as possible.
- Most prefer to be called 'mature' or 'senior citizens'. The least preferred descriptions are 'pensioners', 'elderly' and 'older people'.
- Almost two-thirds believe the media almost always portrays older people in a negative way.
- Compared with a similar survey in Europe, Australia's senior citizens have, in general, a more positive outlook.

Older Australians therefore want to be given a greater chance to contribute to the community, by passing on their knowledge and skills, and by having a say on political, social and cultural issues. Older people are saying they want to be heard and that they are worth listening to.

Our sense of completeness can enhance with the years, for we can be authentically ourselves. As the veteran feminist Betty Friedan told a Melbourne audience, all the experiences she has had over a lifetime are a part of her: 'I am myself at this stage. I have never felt so free. I am not growing old. I am simply growing older.'

This book is more than a checklist of how to go about growing older. It is a kind of compendium of comment and information to dip into at any time. It contains reflections, observations, advice, warnings, and it also faces the downsides that are part of life. There is no dogma, no nonsensical belief that the going will always be smooth; it is how we face rejection, disappointment and our own vulnerability that makes us whole, mature human beings. Maturity can come only with experience, and experience is what those nearing fifty have in abundance.

The material that follows is mainly culled from the writer's own life experience, from her association with the Life Planning Foundation of Australia (formerly the Early Planning for Retirement Association), from her reading and from those who are already in this field, helping people recognise the need to face their future, now.

You will read about that ubiquitous topic, career change, about retrenchment and retirement, about the grieving process that is part of all change. Our financial security is important, but this is only the foundation on which we build our tomorrows.

The notion of leisure, and how to use it creatively, forms an important segment of the book. Then there is the question of one's family, the other half, the grown children, the dependent parent. There are major issues of health — the proper balance of the physical, mental and spiritual. Some of the special questions facing rural Australians are canvassed. Divorce, repartnering and coping with stepfamilies are also lively issues for many people in their middle years. There are options about housing and more besides. Finally, there is an honest approach to the fact that ultimately we are going to die.

Take time to read the book, and prepare to take action! If you do, you will grow, and you will change. Remember the wisdom of the writer Virginia Woolf: she did not believe in ageing, she believed in forever altering one's aspect to the sun. We fifty-somethings believe there can be much that is new, fresh and exhilarating if we engage the future with a sense of hope and purpose.

1
Early planning

No-one should have to ask plaintively, with the poet T.S. Eliot, 'Where is the life we have lost?' Planning should be a lifetime activity. 'Later' is often too late, and can have tragic consequences. The idea of looking ahead can nevertheless be daunting to some, especially to those forty- and fifty-somethings who are reaching or have reached the peak of their careers. 'Life is busy enough', they will say. 'The present is so full, so demanding, there is no time left for tomorrow.'

We are not asking for tomorrow to take over from today; rather we are suggesting that those very people take just a little time to dream, to give time to thinking about themselves in one year, five years, a decade from now. Where do I want to be? With whom do I want to be? What will interest, excite, inspire me?

> Take just a little time to dream: Where do I want to be? With whom do I want to be? What will interest, excite, inspire me?

Such questions need not take long. If you go to work by public transport, for instance, you could spend that time reading this book, jotting down ideas, answering questions and giving yourself some challenges for the future. You owe yourself this luxury!

Take time to dream

Over the meal in the evening, instead of turning on the television news, the family could have a brain-storming, imagining themselves a decade hence. Would they be together? Here or elsewhere? Whose secret dreams are yet to be fulfilled? Have they the courage to spell out the desires nearest their hearts?

We are not ready to speak about that awful word 'retirement', although it has to be faced sooner rather than later. For the moment we are addressing the 'pre-retirees' (an awful word), people in their forties and fifties who have already experienced various transitions and have passed through the gateway to middle age. Leaving school, gaining the first job, accreditation at one's trade, graduation at college or university, marriage, having children, illness, losing a family member, all have been major life experiences. Even changes in the workplace may have been traumatic, yet in retrospect we have managed them, more or less capably. All have added to our store of experience.

If the pre-retiree lists the significant events in his or her life to date, some may well include work and career, others will relate to family, others perhaps to educational goals, some maybe to sadness or failure. Some retirement planning counsellors suggest you write down these marker points, and how you felt about each, both at the time and in retrospect. What did each mean to you? What motivated you at that point? Were they growing points or setbacks in your career, to your personality? Would you react to them differently now? Who mattered most in your life at each significant event?

> Can you anticipate any meaningful events beyond what the world calls 'retirement'?

Given that you may have twenty, thirty or forty more years of life, it is clear there will be further significant events. You are not much more than half-way along your lifeline! Can you anticipate any meaningful events beyond what the world calls 'retirement'?

We hope such questions will encourage you to give time to yourself, about your future self. Above all else, you must not DRIFT into the future with feelings of loneliness, isolation, self-pity or obsolescence. Such negative outcomes are not for the person who looks ahead and plans.

Financial planning

It would be natural to consider first your financial base, and so let's make some general statements right now. Detailed advice to suit your personal needs is readily available from a host of professional sources. In the workforce, you may well be involved in some form of superannuation or other preretirement package. Superannuation is long term and usually has a predictable result at a predetermined age. A preretirement or a retirement package can be offered suddenly and at the employer's initiative. You may have sought advice about this from within your organisation, and from your banker, credit union or financial consultant. You will probably need more.

The general advice to every reader is simple: take time and care in choosing your financial advisers — be as selective as you would be in choosing a doctor; beware of free advice and the hard sell; note how long the company or consultant has been in business; seek out only those with a good reputation and take note of word-of-mouth comments, especially on such issues as follow-up service and understanding of your particular needs. It is often better to have an adviser on a salary than one on commissions.

The Financial Planning Association of Australia produces a consumer guide to selecting a financial adviser called *Don't Kiss Your Money Goodbye*.✱ It is a simple introduction to what questions you should ask and what you need to know, and it is free and available on request. Remember you are always entitled to ask your adviser what brokerage he or she will receive on each of the products recommended to you, and this may help to identify any possible source of bias.

> Find advice that is structured and meaningful to you.

✱ For complete details of all resources mentioned in this book — indicated by this symbol ✱ — see the 'Useful resources' list.

The key point is *your* understanding. Don't be flummoxed by the jargon. Find advice that is structured and meaningful to you, so that you are comfortable in assessing your own position. Noel Whittaker, the Queensland financial adviser who writes a weekly column in twenty newspapers and who broadcasts as well, assures us that accumulating wealth for retirement, then keeping it secure for retirement, is still possible for those *who make the effort* to learn what to do. That is why Whittaker calls the years after sixty 'the years of fulfilment'!

As far back as 1953 a survey of a graduating class of business students at Harvard University found that only ten per cent of that class left with any set goals, and only three per cent had taken the trouble to write down those goals. Twenty years later, those members of the group who had goals were found to have succeeded on all levels, personally through their health and happiness, and professionally through their level of wealth, in ways that were more successful than the other ninety per cent. More importantly, those further three per cent who had written goals were even more significantly successful than the rest.

Stuart Morris, who was in charge of superannuation for Victoria's State Electricity Commission in the 1950s, was staggered to find how many widows had no idea of their entitlement benefits. He educated himself in the intricacies of social service benefits, and from 1958–70 became the widows' advocate, at a time when the SEC was building up to about 20000 personnel in the Latrobe Valley, which had the heaviest density of SEC families.

In 1966 he presented what was to prove a watershed address to the annual national conference of the Association of Superannuation Funds of Australia, covering associated human interest problems. This address, circulated among 155 representatives of Australian companies and organisations, was so pertinent to the times that Sir Willis Connolly, as SEC Chairman and Chairman of Super-Fund Trustees, declared it to be official policy for the Commission. Retirement planning was therefore deemed to have its first formal *imprimatur* in this country.

The early 1970s saw a rising awareness about the need to plan for retirement, or for an earlier crisis. Not only were some employers arranging seminars for staff, to help bring this issue into sharper focus, but medical and social researchers were being given space in the media on the same topic.

Some catchy headlines in the Australian press emphasised the same message. 'How to make a new life from your last great crisis – retirement' was a two-page headline in the *National Times* in 1973. Dr Gary Andrews, medical superintendent of the Lidcombe Hospital in Sydney and a recognised authority on retirement, saw Australia's negative attitudes rooted in our concepts of the aged, and especially in the growth of nursing homes. He could see the increasing interest in euthanasia as an extension of these attitudes, and deplored the fact that if Australians thought of retirement at all, they thought of it only in terms of financial provision, or in vague generalisations in which retirement was largely to do with non-work.

The Inter-church Trade and Industry Mission (ITIM), founded in 1972, studied the experience and statistical analysis of more than fifty leading authorities here and overseas, and established that many Australians were failing to enjoy their retirement because of lack of planning. ITIM advised that the situation could be avoided for present employees if company management implemented schemes to educate staff for this radical change. Stuart Morris contributed to the production of ITIM's retirement planning manual, *People and Retirement*. It challenged private and public organisations on three major issues:

- to become more enlightened as to the needs of individuals approaching retirement
- to recognise the need for, and importance of, counselling
- to do something about it.

The manual stressed that the wife of a retired man would have to adjust as much to her husband's retirement as he himself. (The plight of couples unaccustomed to spending twenty-four hours in each other's company largely remains uncharted territory.) A number of employer and union journals promoted the ITIM booklet, which featured 'the Three Rs' of the modern industrial scene: retirement, retrenchment and redundancy.

For the most part, the problem was more acute in metropolitan areas. Country people were usually more self-reliant; 'they had fish, a football, friends, were territorial and terribly independent anyway'. Country people had most of their time allocated, they had learned how to live on less and fill their lives, the hard way.

Pointers for successful retirement

A mentor of the Early Planning for Retirement Association (established 1972) at this time was Professor Alistair Heron, a British psychologist who brought his experience of retirement planning when he came to the University of Melbourne. Heron's five points for a successful retirement were:

- an adequate income substantially above subsistence level
- compatible friendships
- one or more absorbing interests and hobbies
- comfortable housing, and
- a positive philosophy of life.

In no time the EPRA was persuading employers to conduct seminars for staff up to ten years before their expected retirement, and the benefits were two-way. By encouraging and assisting employees to plan their retirement, employers found, among other benefits, the retention of skilled employees and a decrease in turnover and training costs. There were also more efficient work practices as a result of improved morale and performance of older employees, along with the maintenance of a positive working environment for all staff.

Because there was virtually no published material in Australia at that time to help prepare people for retirement, the board of

EPRA put together a kit that has proved a boon to thousands both before and after retirement. It is now distributed under the new, more appropriate name given to the former EPRA, the Life Planning Foundation of Australia.*

As this topic has lately been recognised as a matter of great importance for the wellbeing of society, useful books written for Australians are now appearing on the market. Some of the titles are noted in the useful resources list at the back of this book.

Age discrimination unlawful

In recent years, most Australian states have made discrimination on the basis of age unlawful, and/or have prohibited compulsory retirement. A basic reason is the need to protect the human rights of those who wish to continue working past the traditional retirement age. Some are still not covered by superannuation, some need to maintain their income level, and, from a national point of view, their continuance in the workforce eases the strain on Social Security. That the skills and experience of older people should be used productively is uncontested. On the other hand there should be no compulsion for people to remain at work. Some of course are obsessed with work and will continue with no cease-by date in mind; others will cheerfully take up the leisure and alternative opportunities offered outside the workplace.

> That the skills and experience of older people should be used productively is uncontested.

Equal Opportunity legislation to prohibit discrimination on the ground of age was introduced in New South Wales in 1977. The provision only commenced operation in 1994. The Act makes it unlawful to discriminate against a person on the ground of age in the workplace, in access to public places, in education, in the provision of goods and services, in accommodation and in registered clubs. There are a number of reasonable exceptions, such as employment in a private household, partnerships of less than six people, educational institutions that require students to be above a particular age, holiday tours for people of a particular age, and others. The New South Wales legislation also contains provisions prohibiting compulsory retirement on the basis of age.

Legislation is now in place in New South Wales, Queensland, South Australia, Western Australia, the ACT and Victoria that prohibits compulsory retirement.

All this must have heartened the Victorian Senator Kay Patterson, who in June 1995 introduced, for the second time, a private Bill to remind the Federal government of its five-year-old promise to remove age discrimination from the Australian Public Service. 'To be denied employment opportunities solely on the basis of age, without regard to ability, qualifications or experience, is no less offensive than discrimination on the basis of sex, race or religion', she told the Senate. 'There is no arbitrary point in life where one can say you are no longer a productive and worthwhile member of the workforce. There is no magic in the age of sixty-five – rather it is an age related to an earlier era when life expectancy was less and healthy ageing less common.'

> There is no magic in the age of sixty-five

Senator Patterson countered the argument that a longer stay at work might have an impact on young job-seekers by stating that it was a philosophically flawed argument to discriminate against one group in order to promote the rights of another group. That type of argument, she continued, was used to preclude married women from participating in the workforce.

(The Federal Human Rights and Equal Opportunity Commission in 1990 formally advised the Federal Attorney-General on the need for further legislation against age discrimination.)

The whole issue of preretirement education is now on the international agenda. Our changing demography is forcing serious study of older people's lives, for they no longer fit the stereotype of frailty and approaching senility. Thankfully, they are coming to be seen more as contributors to, than receivers from, society.

Professor Hal Kendig, director of the Lincoln Gerontology Centre for Education and Research, sees good planning and continuity as keys to personal success in old age. A fulfilling and meaningful life well into our later years is largely dependent, he has been quoted as saying, on the society we create and the external messages we receive from family, friends and the media. Importantly, it all comes down to the sorts of choices we make in our younger years. Dr Kendig states:

> It all comes down to the sorts of choices we make in our younger years.

> How things turn out for us in old age depends very much on the kind of investments we make in mid-life. That is not only financial but emotional, social and how we look after our own health. The trajectory we set in our twenties, thirties and forties very much determines what we are doing in old age.

So let us see how to get that trajectory in motion! The future does not present a world without a map. It presents a map on which you can plan your next adventures in the world.

In short ...

1 Take time now to read about retirement, to jot down ideas, to pose and answer your own questions and to set yourself future challenges.

2 Brainstorm ideas with the family about your respective lives in ten years. Be imaginative, visionary and courageous.

3 List the marker points in your life to date. Note how each affected you at the time, and how you feel about each one now.

4 Do not allow yourself simply to drift towards the future.

5 Seek reliable professional financial advice to suit your personal needs.

6 Take as much care and time to choose a financial adviser as you would choose a doctor.

7 Take advantage of any preretirement counselling that is offered at your place of employment.

8 Keep in mind that a full and meaningful life in later years depends on the choices you make now, and that one of these choices could be whether you wish to retire, or to keep working.

2
Humanising the workplace

As shown in chapter 1, some enlightened workplaces do provide for human services focusing away from the job. Such services include libraries, swimming pools, sports areas and other recreation facilities. The humanisation of the workplace is all to the good.

Some companies and many departments in the public sector have become increasingly committed to helping employees in their lives beyond the job. Organisations such as the Inter-church Trade and Industry Mission (ITIM), and firms specialising in outplacement, are part of this growing network of care on and beyond the job. People in their forties and fifties are of particular concern to these professional counsellors and advisers.

> Some companies and many departments in the public sector have become increasingly committed to helping employees in their lives beyond the job.

Work and families

It may be a truism that the family is the silent partner in employee relations, but it was good to see the family achieve centre stage as a field of national concern when the Australian Institute of Family Studies (AIFS) was established in 1980. Dr Don Edgar was its founding director, and quickly gained a high profile for the Institute, and for himself, as an articulate and co-operative spokesperson on matters to do with the family. The Institute's journal *Family Matters* remains an important resource.

The three-year Australian Living Standards Study, funded by the Federal government in 1991 gave the AIFS the opportunity to interview 5000 families in twelve distinct areas of Australia. The study provided valuable material on a whole range of family issues. Of interest to those around fifty years of age was the support given by grandparents. This not only involved child minding while parents were at work, but also emotional, financial and practical support.

The study also showed that those families most under pressure were at extreme ends of the socio-economic scale, with high flyers working long hours and those most vulnerable in low-paid jobs having inflexible employment arrangements. On the other hand, the study found large corporations developing 'family friendly' arrangements with flexible work hours and providing permission for leave from work for one hour when necessary.

Counselling for change

ITIM, established in 1960 to promote the wellbeing of people in the workplace, helps industry to focus on the fundamental value of the person, always with an unswerving commitment to human dignity.

Despite the negativity shown within industry towards the Church, ITIM's chaplains are welcomed for their pastoral skill and practical compassion. These chaplains are articulating the Church's public ministry to a sector of the population who may never set foot inside a church, and are delivering the Church's values to an estimated quarter of a million Australians who come into contact with a chaplain each week (not only at work, but in hospitals, schools and prisons).

With change now an integral aspect of work in many public sector organisations, ITIM counsellors conduct training and group counselling programmes where the shedding of staff, or changing roles, inevitably make the workplace different from what it has been in the past. The counselling process has become more urgent in recent years, as staff, particularly those in middle management, have seen the onset of profound change. Helping staff to find the ability to cope by means of a heightened sense of identity and self-esteem is a particular challenge for the chaplain.

> The counselling process has become more urgent in recent years, as staff, particularly those in middle management, have seen the onset of profound change.

The issues facing workers aged fifty-plus include those of change and transition. As they grow older, many people will face their first real illness, and become aware of their vulnerability. They will want to reappraise their life, and its meaning. The 'making meaning' questions become increasingly important:

- Is that all there is to life?
- My children are growing up, leaving home, and do not need me — what is my function now?
- What is the point of work and routine?
- What shall I do with the rest of my life?
- Do I still matter?

Looking to retirement, and accepting redundancy at fifty-plus are challenging issues for many. Are there ways to finding fulfilment in life other than through paid work? Some are anxious to take redundancy packages without thinking through all the losses they may experience: workmates, routine, identity, social relationships. They also need encouragement and skilled assistance in continuing their personal growth, and their search for meaningful alternatives.

Outplacement

ITIM tends to complement the work of outplacement consultants such as Morgan and Banks,* Australia's largest human resources organisation. Outplacement was developed in the United States over twenty years ago, to assist managers who were hit by restructuring and the reductions of middle-management positions. The practical and structured approach of outplacement is entirely focused on helping clients succeed. Even though an economic recovery is now under way in Australia, it does not mean the end of restructuring, for companies and government departments are continually looking for ways to be more efficient, and therefore more competitive.

Alan Simpson, a senior outplacement consultant with Morgan and Banks, begins with the premise that anyone retrenched can get a job. There is no such thing as an unemployable person, he states, provided he or she wants a job, is prepared to listen and take advice on how to go about seeking a job, provided a realistic goal is set and they work hard in the search.

> There is no such thing as an unemployable person provided he or she wants a job, a realistic goal is set and they work hard in the search.

'People who have been retrenched tend, in retrospect, to forget how upset they were at the time', Alan Simpson states. 'Their responses vary enormously of course, but the moment they are given the news is usually uncomfortable for everyone. There is a lot of anxiety on both sides of the desk; in fact most managers say giving another employee notice is the worst aspect of their job.'

If one works in a medium to large enterprise, there is an excellent chance these days that outplacement consultants will be used during a period of retrenchment. Managers are trained to break the news, for they certainly need advice in such a difficult situation.

Generally, the outplacement consultant is present the day the axe falls, to begin the counselling process immediately. 'It is not a rescue service, nor are we magicians', Alan Simpson maintains. 'Once the initial hurdle is overcome, people are advised to leave the company quickly and we put them through a process of self-assessment.'

They are given a battery of tests to determine their transferable skills, values and 'career drivers' (that is, the different things that motivate people). It is a fairly lengthy process. But out of it all comes their 'ideal next job' options. The person has spent time considering the perfect next job, and the ideal company. Once he or she has gone through all this they become involved in a *targeted* job search.

It is useless to apply for every job advertised in the newspapers, Alan Simpson maintains. (Have you seen the occasional job seeker on TV with 300 rejection slips, and still no job?) Interview skills are immensely important, as are the applicant's letters and a careful resumé of past experience. When finally presenting before a selection panel, those who are prepared in every way usually get the job they themselves have chosen!

> Take your career in your own hands.
> Don't settle for second best.

There are special problems for executives – usually men – right at the top. They are assumed to be self-sufficient, but as Alan Simpson states, there is nobody who cannot benefit from some advice at the right level.

For those who are not perfectly placed in the right job, Alan Simpson has some further advice. Change it! Take your career in your own hands. Don't settle for second best.

Strategies for successful people

Anne Evans, for twenty-six years a career public servant in the field of human resources consulting and now a private consultant, writes and speaks about the fear and guilt that many experience in times of recession. Some, she states, literally talk themselves into disaster; their worry is at a level that outweighs their ability to manage themselves. Their greatest danger is intense, helpless worrying that only makes their worst fears more likely to become reality.

Others who know they will survive, relatively unhurt, have developed strategies to help them maintain and support a positive outlook that will lead them to seize new opportunities. Here are the strategies Anne Evans identifies among successful people:

- They lead balanced lives.
- They accept themselves.
- They have a playful attitude to work, and to themselves.
- They are truly interested in, curious about and fascinated by their field of endeavour.
- They innovate.
- They enter into strategic alliances.
- Whatever work they do, to these people their work is a constant challenge.
- They add value to whatever they tackle.

All these attributes can be cultivated, Anne Evans claims. If in doubt, she advises some 'mental calisthenics' to loosen up. Six ways are suggested:

- Learn something new.
- Deliberately break your routines.
- Practise active listening.
- Teach something to somebody else.
- Select a topic that has an element of controversy, take a viewpoint opposite to one you favour, carefully prepare your position, and defend it.
- Look after your health.
- Stop worrying – it is debilitating physically and mentally.

As Anne states, worry fills your mind only if there is room for it. We shall consider the whole question of health in later chapters.

In short ...

1 Accept that change has become an integral aspect of the workplace.

2 Take advantage of training and counselling programmes designed to help staff heighten their sense of identity and self-esteem in an uncertain environment.

3 Many people aged fifty-plus face their first real illness, and this might be a reminder of your vulnerability.

4 If you are facing retirement or redundancy, ask yourself: Is paid work the only way to achieve fulfilment in life?

5 Be prepared to listen to and accept advice on how to go about seeking a new job. Set realistic goals and work hard in the search.

6 Develop your letter-writing, resumé and interview skills.

7 Beware the danger of worrying yourself into disaster. Maintain a positive outlook and be prepared to seize new opportunities.

8 Practise the six ways to cultivate the attributes for success.

3
Transition – to what?

Many more women today are reaching senior positions in the workforce in their early forties. This situation has evolved quickly and the pace of the evolution is accelerating. To reach these positions many women have had to forsake a great deal, as traditionally men have been expected to do. Friendships have been put on hold, if not lost forever, free time is an opportunity to catch up on more work, even health and fitness are sacrificed in pursuit of the goal. Work has become, literally, a full-time vocation.

> Caught between sticky floors and glass ceilings, they wonder if there is more to life. They are looking for joy, renewal and balance. They have become exhausted, cynical, even robotic.

Meredith Fuller, a Melbourne psychologist who is a career change specialist, is seeing 'a swell of people in their forties' whose professional careers appear to have peaked. Caught between sticky floors and glass ceilings, they wonder if there is more to life. These are the kind of questions she hears in her counselling sessions:

- Is this as far as I can get?
- Has it been worth the sacrifice?
- Have I alienated myself and my loved ones?

They are looking for joy, renewal and balance, Meredith explains. They have become exhausted, cynical, even robotic. This latter symptom shows itself particularly in men: they are a bit frozen, disconnected. The counsellor finds these clients having to deal with loss and disappointment issues, and fearful about the way the rest of their life may be heading. While men may be disappointed with where they have ended up, women may have peaked too soon, with nowhere else to go.

Too often, these people turn around and begin a new cycle, repeating the same treadmill they have tried to escape. They've been climbing up the wrong mountain! How do they stay energised and remain in the workforce? They need to learn to nourish what reserves of energy they have to construct an alternative career that will sustain them. They may take a 'transition' job, or several part-time roles, while they retrain or begin their own business, or allow themselves some 'contemplation' time to renew their lives and begin to hear their inner desires.

They need to begin addressing other parts of themselves, surrendering the old, partnering the new, moving, in Meredith's telling phrase, 'from woe to wonder'. 'You must connect with those parts of yourself you've neglected or never valued, or which have never been touched', she explains.

'High flyers' will find such a challenge very difficult, for it may mean significant surrender. Meredith quotes an unhappy surgeon who had become disillusioned with his high level, highly responsible place in a distinguished profession. He was feeling like a lonely carpenter instead of a healer. Having been helped to acknowledge other untapped parts of his own personality, he had the courage to surrender his position at the operating table and take up studies in theology. He is now a missionary, has a small general practice, owns a small farm and enjoys his animals. All this has been at a cost, of course. His former colleagues cannot understand the change and have therefore dropped out of his life, and his material income has been dramatically diminished. The tension of the previous job has gone forever, and he now enjoys harmonious relationships he did not share in the upper echelons of medicine. His capacity to surrender was the crucial step in his move to a new life.

People who have been totally focused on the one occupation, but who now seek an alternative career path must be prepared to 'play', to explore different things and test a range of activities and lifestyle possibilities until they find a skill that 'fits'. One counsellor suggests cold-bloodedly making fresh contacts with a whole variety of *people*. Many will be dropped by the wayside, for such friendships will inevitably be short-term. Some, however, can prove fruitful and lead to hitherto unthought-of interests and activities. This counsellor suggests, when meeting new persons, that one answer differently to the stock question: 'What do you do?' Rather than reply, 'I'm a bank clerk', 'teacher' or whatever, one might reply, 'Well, I'm into hang gliding and other things, trying to define who I am and what I value!'

Trying alternative roles

One needs to be primitive, experimental, even clumsy, in trying out a different role. You must allow yourself to make mistakes. I like the story of the famous plastic surgeon who knew he must find an alternative interest as his time in the operating theatre was drawing to a close. Among other things he took painting lessons. The otherwise skilled fingers were very clumsy indeed with a paintbrush for a while, but he loved the smell of paint and the freedom to choose where to go outdoors. Now he spends most of his time painting, he has had several exhibitions and is proud of his modest sales.

> One needs to be primitive, experimental, even clumsy, in trying out a different role. You must allow yourself to make mistakes.

It is a pity there are not more people who operate in the spiral mode. These people have a unifying theme throughout their lives, such as the process of teaching, organising or problem solving. They are constantly encompassing new things that enable them to evolve, and remain curious forever. Psychologists give these people the tag 'multiple role definition'. The majority, however, are not in spiral mode. Far more are one-dimensional, defining themselves by a core identity or single focus, whether it be as a parent or a business amazon. Having seen the last child leave, or having seen their career peak reached, the same devastation and rage can set in because they do not have a range of roles or aspects to the self to define who they are.

There is no quick-fix escape for them, but they can be helped. 'Always have a guide when you're going on a journey', Meredith Fuller advises. 'The guide will be a witness to your story and help you through some sort of ceremonial way of letting go and embracing new possibilities.'

> There are also thousands who find they are neither visible nor valued in their place of work. They too must be helped to recover their self-esteem.

Many women find it nourishing to start telling their story to themselves, to write a sequential biography, no matter how halting, of their life to date. In this way they are negotiating who they are and how they feel about the world. They have the luxury of sitting and reflecting quietly, and sometimes this leads to a truly creative insight. Out of this reflection, no matter how tangled, they will draw some threads to identify who they are becoming.

Again, they must be able to tolerate their clumsiness – and their pain – in exploring the past, but they will regain the confidence to see that they can drive their life forward. For some, the very act of writing arouses a desire to study (the issue of returning to learning will be pursued in detail in a later chapter).

There are also thousands who find they are neither visible nor valued in their place of work. They too must be helped to recover their self-esteem and either locate a more satisfying environment, or learn ways to begin modifying their current work role and organisation culture. Retraining for a new role or an entirely different career, through evening courses at community learning centre, TAFE college or university can open up a wonderland of possibilities.

While many people in their forties and fifties need to simplify their lives while still at work, the opposite can also happen. With age and experience, they can become more active. A man had a dull but secure job in a small tie factory in a dreary inner suburb and managed to provide himself and his wife with a pleasant home, and to educate two children to tertiary level. He directed his creative energy in his spare time into building up the Boy Scout movement in the burgeoning outer eastern suburbs. He had leadership skills, wooed fathers and mothers into both uniformed and lay areas of the movement, cajoled land out of municipal councils for Scout halls, and was an impressive persuader in getting local citizens to serve on committees. All that was twenty years ago. The Cubs and Scouts of that generation are now parents themselves and the need for youth activities has moved to still more distant suburbs. So the former tie manufacturer, former District Commissioner for Scouts, has lately directed his interest to returned servicemen and women and is one of the dynamic people behind the building of extensive RSL quarters in his home suburb. He is a happy man.

Acknowledge the crisis and act

There are some people who do not enjoy working with others. Looking elsewhere for more congenial workmates does not necessarily provide the panacea. Meredith Fuller recalls a former nun in a teaching role who frankly admitted she did not like people. This woman was eventually forced into taking a retrenchment package, and part of it she spent sensibly on getting professional advice. Now self-employed, she is running her own small farm, enjoys a wine appreciation course and loves starting a rigorous business in her late fifties where she can be alone. Here was a case of dropping the notion she had to get on with people. This woman has not looked back

> Whenever the crisis in mid-life comes, it is most important to acknowledge it, and seek ways of getting support.

since making the move to the farm, something she always wanted to do, but had been concerned that to be acceptable she should work with people.

People with project management skills or leadership skills may certainly feel a deep sense of loss of influence or *camaraderie* if they choose to move to a lower affiliation. Loneliness for one's peers can be very real. A high-powered executive in the building industry was finding the job an immense strain. It was taking a physical toll, and questions like 'Is this all there is to life?' dominated his thinking. With counselling, he too was able to get in touch with the healer in himself. He trained as a physiotherapist, dropped the big ego, and now finds life eminently satisfying and meaningful. He has regular mentor and networking meetings with colleagues to avoid loneliness or burnout.

Whenever the crisis in mid-life comes, it is most important to acknowledge it, and seek ways of getting support. A good starting point is the yellow pages in the telephone directory, which lists practitioners under 'Psychologists', and the Vocational Guidance section. Psychologists can also administer vocational tests to help identify skills, job preferences, workstyle interests and career suitabilities.

Numbness may set in for a while, and this must be allowed space and time to disappear. Searching the 'Positions Vacant' columns in the newspapers, rushing around with a dozen job applications, is not wise. This is the period for reflection, to look at what has been ignored in one's own life, to get past that feeling of being driven or trapped. It's the time people talk about 'wanting to get out of gaol', while not knowing the route to freedom.

Here is another word of warning. Do not expect the family to be the only ones to hold all this pain for you. Talking to people with like experience, and/or a counsellor, ensures that one does not 'contaminate' personal relationships, as families may be overwhelmed by the strain and may lack the resources to help.

Make every opportunity to get advice, even if you don't feel ready at the time. Obviously, having a job is important, but quickly jumping into the wrong job is the wrong kind of security at any age, let alone at mid-career. Bartering a skill with another has possibilities, for in such a way both can give something precious of themselves to the other.

Sometimes two part-time jobs, even of unequal interest or merit, can be helpful if the hours can be successfully juggled. Working out what one can tolerate is the requisite here. One needs to be mindful, too, of the labour market. One should look at the nexus between what one can do and what society needs.

Importantly, we must recognise there is no such thing as a perfect job. Some declare that fifty-five per cent satisfaction rate is as much as one can expect, while others consider sixty-five per cent as a good balance.

Most interviewed several years down the track say 'being made redundant, or deciding on a career change is the best thing that ever happened to me'. They say they are happier, feel more vibrant, vital and fulfilled. 'Sure you confront a pit or hole at first, but you clamber out to a bigger, more lush terrain!'

> Importantly, we must recognise there is no such thing as a perfect job.

Bad learning about life

Christopher Langan-Fox, a Melbourne psychologist, believes our modern *malaise* is born out of several generations of bad learning about what life is about. 'A lot of lessons for living seem to be in short supply', he states. 'Too many people in their forties are still striving to fulfil the demands of eighteen-year-olds. It's time forty-year-olds started thinking like forty-year-olds.' The speed of change and the mechanisms of the 'me, now' generation have overwhelmed many people. The basic issues of problem solving, delaying satisfaction, understanding of reality and truth, seem to have been lost. Many people arrive at forty bereft of life's tolls and meaning.

'They lack mission and self-discipline', says Langan-Fox. 'Mission has been taken over as a corporate term. Companies have mission statements. But it is a theological term. Individuals should have the missions relevant to them as individuals.'

He suggests this age group take time to look at how they have dealt with life so far. Upon careful examination they will find they have done a great many things they can claim as achievements. They have got over many hurdles which, in retrospect, seem to have been daunting indeed.

Why not construct a *curriculum vitae*, not as a boast of your accomplishments, but as a review? Look at segments of your working life, say in two-to-five-year periods, and see what projects have given you cause for pride. What qualities in yourself were responsible for that success? Was it a gift for initiation, for creativity, for listening, for analysis, for team work? These skills can be redeployed in a myriad of ways!

> It is your desires for the future that matter here. At a deep level, it is what you want to happen that you make happen.

Langan-Fox invites his clients to write their own obituary, forty years hence. This given them the opportunity to dream. Adventures they hardly dare mention are 'permitted'. The first forty years of the obituary are of course factual, for they have already been lived, but the next unlived half gives you a licence to make it all up. It is your desires for the future that matter here. At a deep level, it is what you want to happen that you make happen. Sadly, the belief that you cannot do something is all too often proven by one's inactivity: it is a self-fulfilling prophecy.

Langan-Fox specialises in outplacement, that is finding new roles for people who have been retrenched. These clients are suddenly confronted with the reality that they have pursued a pattern largely defined by others. They have been cast into a role where the expectations of others, especially of the boss or one's peers, are paramount. Sacrifices of all kinds have been made to meet these expectations, and one justifies them as being 'for the good of my family'.

Corporate life is not 'enjoyed' by most men, Langan-Fox declares firmly. It is something that 'has to be done', and if one takes that route, 'liking' it is not a necessary condition. And women are fast learning the same truth. The push forward and upward, defining one's self solely in terms of that occupation, is a great trap, because suddenly the question arises: 'What is it all for?' The desire for upward career mobility has suddenly gone. Ambition has become sour, and the goal one set out to achieve was set by a person of eighteen. The glittering job at forty-five, so alluring to the eighteen-year-old, is an illusion. After all, what does an eighteen-year-old know, even a bright one? The golden chalice is not to be found in the board room, nor on the top floor, nor behind the desk in the office with the largest piece of carpet.

A whole lot of attitudes must therefore be undone. The first step in seeking help is to acknowledge it is needed. You must give yourself permission to act. If you respect yourself, you must help yourself to invest in your own future. Tell yourself you are worth spending a bit of money on! If a loan is the only way to pay for this, then surprise the bank manager and declare you are at last doing something for yourself.

The adolescent Australian male

Unfortunately men do not seek personal help as women do, yet it is always available. Mothers particularly have socialised sons to do things by themselves. Langan-Fox acknowledges 'the aggressively resentful, adolescent Australian male temperament' is distrustful of professional advice. He persists nevertheless. In the outplacement field, many firms will co-operate with specialists in providing suitable counselling for employees on the way out. This is an ideal vehicle for men. They may be counselled in groups, or they may prefer to be interviewed alone. Either way, they should find the outplacement consultant helpful as he or she takes them first through the grieving process that must be faced.

The consultant will work through the familiar flatness or depression as the loss messages really dawn, then the outpouring of anger can be unleashed. Only after that process, when one capitulates and accepts the situation, can one reconstruct one's attitudes and values.

Langan-Fox believes strongly in fantasy. Everything starts with a dream, a desire. It is the power that propels us to do something. The Eiffel Tower is there because someone wanted it there. It did not appear magically, or by accident.

So, whether one has reached a crisis in middle age, or life continues smoothly enough, there remains the ever-present requirement to look ahead and plan. Adjustment to change can be so much less painful if it is gradual! A British film entitled 'A Time to Look Forward' has been going around retirement seminars for some years, and it shows how four people cope when retirement finally happens. The first is a supervisor who decides well in advance to train in carpentry, a hobby that has always attracted him. He buys tools while still in the workforce, and in due course the hobby helps to supplement his superannuation. The next is a single woman who decides to move to the country, only to find she is too far removed from friends and former interests. Third is a former employee who has sufficient superannuation and capital, but is bored, and now finds a mixture of voluntary and a little paid work rewarding. Fourth is a dreamer who wants to move to a bleak seaside village, without his wife's concurrence! There are lots of lessons to be learned from this.

> Everything starts with a dream, a desire. It is the power that propels us to do something. The Eiffel Tower is there because someone wanted it there.

Dry rot in the tree of life

The main lesson, surely, is to think of the traps ahead, and consider how they might be avoided. A motto sometimes introduced by speakers in this context is: 'To finish one's working life, sit back and let the world go by is the equivalent of introducing *dry rot* into the *tree of life*. Another often used is a throwaway line by the American financier Bernard Baruch: 'A man can't retire his experience – he must use it'.

As well as seeking personal help, one can find much wisdom, solace and practical advice in current literature. The healthy mature-aged and the elderly have become a new topic of study in recent decades. One of the most successful interpreters of the crises that can confront mature adults is the American psychologist Gail Sheehy. Her two landmark books, *Passages* and *Pathfinders*,* have sold in millions.

Sheehy is a positive writer, showing how life crises can be an opportunity for creative change. The best lives are those lived by people who let go old roles and find a renewal of purpose in other roles. She calls the forty-plus period the dangerous years, that period of life (remember Langan-Fox's advice about the adventurous eighteen-year-olds?) that needs re-assessment. They offer the greatest opportunity of one's life for re-assessment.

The fifty-plus years are in Sheehy's terms the refreshed or resigned years, when one has faced the risks of change. Again, it is a time when one can be freed to acknowledge the real person. Any time after the birth of one's first grandchild, in fact, frees us to begin our true education as an adult, discovering who we are and pondering life's meaning. Sheehy has a telling phrase: 'We must be willing to change chairs if we want to grow'.

A comforting finding, after her interviews with thousands of adults across the United States and Europe, is that the most satisfied in maturity have lived through some sadness or unhappiness which they have rated as a crisis. Orientation towards the future, rather than dwelling on the past or present, has been a characteristic these people share.

A striking example of this can be found in the experience of Victor Frankl, a psychiatrist who was imprisoned in one of the

German concentration camps during World War Two. To distract himself from his own misfortune, he studied his fellow prisoners and became intrigued with the question of survival. Why did some succumb, while others did not? He found the answer: having a reason to live. Those who found some meaning in their ordeal, had a far higher chance of surviving than those who continually bemoaned their fate.

The Darwin cyclone experience

A dramatic example of preparedness in the face of tragedy or disaster is given by Jo Wilson, who, with her husband and four-month-old baby, suffered the terror of the Darwin cyclone in the Northern Territory at Christmas time in 1974. Now a lecturer in the fields of women in management, personal development and presentation skills – to name a few – Jo often accepts public speaking engagements on what she calls 'The Winds of Change'.

Based on the Darwin experience, she uses her escape, her realisation of mortality and her future plans as the basis of these talks. Some of her most helpful ideas include:

- Setting goals – and taking action to achieve them.
- Visualisation – day-dreaming, and believing totally in one's capabilities.
- Affirmation – of one's self, with no negative beliefs.
- Setting a time frame – writing plans down, focusing totally, being persistent, realistic and specific.
- Believing in one's self by making positive statements – I am, I have, I do.

So, the best way to make the most of one's tomorrows, while enjoying the present, is to assign an array of self-chosen tasks, and prepare to live in a rhythm between those assignments, recreation and rest. Let us now look at this notion of recreation, and leisure.

In short …

1 Acknowledge the crisis whenever it comes and seek support.

2 Talk to people with experience. Do not expect the family or close friends to bear all your pain.

3 Look at alternatives. Allow yourself time to renew your life. Listen to your inner desires.

4 Be prepared to 'play', to explore and to test other possibilities.

5 Make fresh contacts. They may lead to unthought-of interests and activities.

6 Don't expect to find the perfect job – this is extremely rare.

7 Construct a *curriculum vitae* as a review. See what has caused you the most pride in your working life.

8 The belief that you cannot achieve something can too easily become a self-fulfilling prophesy. Fortunately the opposite is also true. It will happen if you want it to, at a deep level.

4
Leisure and recreation – spending time or using time?

More than 2000 years ago the Greek philosopher, Aristotle, had the wisdom to state that the goal of all education is the wise use of leisure time. A modern American President, Herbert Clark Hoover, perhaps had Aristotle in mind when he declared 'the future of our civilisation does not depend on what we do on the job, but what we do in our life off the job'.

The word 'leisure' has been extraordinarily difficult to define. The Septuagint, the first translation of the Hebrew Bible into Greek, gives us that lovely line in the forty-sixth psalm 'Have leisure and know that I am God'. The King James version is 'Be still, and know that I am God'. Modern Jewish translations say 'Let be, relax, and know that I am God'. The Good News Bible says 'Stop fighting, and know that I am God'! All these translations nevertheless give different insights into the possibilities of leisure. In all of them, there is a sense of surrender, of relief, of the spiritual. The term 'Waiting on the Lord' has its expression in many of the world's religions, exhorting followers to be still, let be, relax, meditate, wonder and marvel.

The anthropologist Margaret Mead used to say that the belief that leisure has to be earned dies hard. There is, as yet, no fully accepted social role for people who have ceased paid work. One must not, however, equate leisure with laziness or idleness. The lazy person is another creature altogether: he or she says 'No' to life. The person with leisure time is able to give an unreserved 'Yes' to life. Perhaps 'free time' is really a better phrase in the context we are using here. Even so, we are not so much considering time on the clock, but time one can call one's own, time one is adapting constructively for life off the job. This kind of time requires an inner capacity to make decisions, to make an effort.

> There is, as yet, no fully accepted social role for people who have ceased paid work.

Sandor Ferenczi, a Hungarian psychiatrist, is said to have coined the phrase 'Sunday neuroses' for the person who simply could not switch off from paid work. (Such a person could never comprehend the dignity, beauty and refreshment of what the Jewish Sabbath truly means.) Rather than enjoy the change from weekday work, this person would either look for another job – 'moonlighting' – or sink into irritability or mild depression. Such a person was not in control of their own life, and could not think creatively beyond the work they were paid to do: clearly a candidate for what another psychiatrist, the American Alexander Reid Martin, called the geriatric ghetto.

Leisure happens within us

Martin was a specialist in the field of leisure time and its uses. Put simply, Martin states that leisure is something that happens within us. You do not go after leisure, leisure comes to you, but *only when the inner and outer conditions of your life are favourable*. If these are in the right balance, then what he calls 'that great and unique potential which belongs only to the field of recreation' can be activated.

Martin writes of 'autonomous effort', an innate capacity that is inner directed, self-initiated and self-determined. It is a virtue that has its own reward. How often does one hear of a person given an award for some outstanding contribution to the wellbeing of others, only to be quoted as saying the task was one of love, a joy to do?

> You do not go after leisure, leisure comes to you, but only when the inner and outer conditions of your life are favourable.

One of the most striking statements I have found in relation to the old question 'What should I do?' comes from Alexander Martin. He advises that 'healthy adaptation to free time in so many instances involves undoing what you have been doing habitually for years'.

One of the lessons learned in the Healthy Lifestyle Weekends sponsored by Active Seniors in Victoria has been the sad fact that many participants had never given themselves a 'wish list', let alone the opportunity to fulfil a wish or two in previous years. Never having joined a club, nor pursued a skill, they had scant confidence in suddenly taking up a project.

Other states have similar recreation associations, and work somewhat differently. Tasmania's Department of Tourism, Sport and Recreation runs a '50 Plus' programme from April to September.* It provides a wide range of healthy lifestyle activities for the older adult population, from abseiling and archery, camel treks and camping, picnics and philately, to walking and weightlifting.

In Tasmania, the School for Seniors* is an exciting new development whose philosophy is to promote learning from others of a similar age, in small friendly groups. A fee of ten dollars per year enables seniors to attend as many centres as they wish.

Tasmania's Older Adults Recreation Strategy wisely combines with youth and other recreation activities – like the '35 Plus' programme – to encourage lifelong activity and participation.

South Australia has a Recreational Association for Older Adults, Queensland and Western Australia organise theirs through their Sport and Recreation Departments, and Queensland's is organised through the Office of Ageing. The common denominator in all states is the value of bringing older people together, both those willing to pursue new interests, and those who co-ordinate and provide the service.

One of the early images of the women's movement in the 1970s was that of a bird in a cage. The cage door was open. It was up to the bird to take wing, and fly through the door.

Obvious actions to facilitate flight in this case include collecting promotional books and pamphlets, listening to the many who speak of their speciality on radio, and following up those enthusiasts who are interviewed in newspapers. Recreationists, skilled experts and practitioners in voluntary organisations are available to answer queries. One can always visit facilities, and write for information. Some of the familiar places where information is stored, awaiting perusal, include local libraries, community information centres and citizens' advice bureaus, municipal recreation departments, community houses and the YWCA.

Some likely objectives

Here are some questions:
- What is going to be different for you between now and five or ten years' hence?
- What are you looking forward to?
- Can you imaginatively project yourself into your own future?
- Can you move into the business of bridge-building, from now into the future, so that instead of retiring *from* something in the next decade, you are moving *to* something?

We are now involved in what has been termed 'The Interval of Query', that time when we need to consider our personal life objectives, or goals. As we mature, we are likely to want to:
- be useful
- stay independent

- help other people
- have plenty of friends
- make our community a better place to live in
- stay in touch with our family
- keep our minds active and alert
- work and earn more money
- keep our good health
- reap the rewards of a lifetime's work.

> Almost any activity can be recreational if it is freely chosen for the enjoyment and inbuilt satisfaction it brings.

Each of these objectives can be threshed out, alone or with a partner, writing down specific ways of achieving them.

Then there is what we call a personal leisure inventory, beginning with the word 'things'. These 'things' can be big or little, and encompass games, hobbies, stocks and shares, creative arts and crafts, sporting interests, politics, community involvement, study and much more. Almost any activity can be recreational if it is freely chosen for the enjoyment and inbuilt satisfaction it brings. Here is the list to check:

- things I do well
- things I enjoy doing alone
- things I enjoy doing with people
- things I would like to continue doing
- things I would like to stop doing
- things I would like to try
- things I like to learn to do more of
- things I would like to do well
- things I enjoy doing that cost less than five dollars
- things I enjoy doing with my partner
- things I enjoy doing with my children
- things I do not enjoy doing with the family
- things that require a risk
- things I would like to share with others
- great experiences I have had
- great experiences I would like to have

While these things can be pursued, or rejected, after our paid working life has ended, one can begin to acquire the skills involved in most of the above while one is still in the workforce. 'Anticipated leisure' may be at the basis of most people's expectations; it is *how* we anticipate that is important. Only by being positive can we happily say 'yes' to the question: '*Will we be ready for retirement when it comes?*'

A worksheet, with a long list of ways of finding satisfaction, is often used in group seminars on the topic of recreation. It is a helpful list. You may like to tick the kind of satisfaction you are seeking, alone or with a partner:

- sharing common interests
- working with my hands
- feeling useful, wanted
- making new friends
- paying my way
- mental stimulation
- feeling life is meaningful
- being independent
- feeling at peace
- having an adventure
- taking a risk
- accepting a challenge
- keeping fit/healthy
- being a participant
- a feeling of mastery
- maintaining self-respect
- having an income
- having authority
- being respected
- feeling important/needed
- learning something new
- being creative
- being contemplative, spiritual
- helping myself

- helping other people
- feeling productive
- maintaining a skill
- being entertained
- being protecting/feeling protected
- giving/receiving affection
- having an influence
- acting spontaneously
- being a spectator
- having insights
- increasing awareness
- appreciating nature
- fun, excitement

How to acquire that sense of motivation and exploration – what Albert Einstein called a holy curiosity – if stagnation has already crept into the psyche is the real challenge.

Here is another exercise: Draw a line across a sheet of paper with your year of birth at the far left and expected year of death at the far right. (It might have to be a nice wide sheet of paper for this!) Indicate on your left line the point where you are now, and mark that point NOW. Indicate the year you expect to 'retire' and mark it R. First, to the left of NOW, list five major events up to this point in your life. To the right list five of the major events, happenings, activities or experiences you hope to enjoy before you die.

On another sheet, list, if you can remember them, the things you wanted most as a child, as a teenager, as an early adult, then your first mid-life crisis and, lastly, what you expect to face upon leaving paid work. These revelations are likely to show both positives and negatives, but hopefully you will record among your future aspirations the acquiring of new skills and new interests. One would not want to see too many notations like isolation, loneliness, wasted time, obsolescence, uselessness, self-pity and depression. New uses of time and fewer family responsibilities, with concrete plans for the future, can dispel these unhappy possibilities.

How to acquire that sense of motivation and exploration – what Albert Einstein called a holy curiosity – if stagnation has already crept into the psyche is the real challenge. To float in a sea of nothingness sounds a horrible alternative to the kind of living we aim to explore.

Another good technique, alongside the questions listed above, is to reflect upon the times one has been so immersed that one's self has been forgotten. Has there been a time when work has not been the driving force? This can be a gate-opener! Has any holiday period been something more than recuperation from work?

In view of the statement by the social researcher, Hugh McKay, that our leisure time is what defines us as Australians, it is appropriate to consider the National Recreation Survey completed in 1991. It showed the top activities enjoyed by Australian men and women fifty-five years and over: watching TV at home; listening to radio; reading; visiting friends and relatives; listening to music; relaxing doing nothing; gardening for pleasure; talking to friends on the telephone for more than fifteen minutes; exercising and keeping fit at home; playing outdoors with children; walking for pleasure; shopping for pleasure; socialising at pubs, clubs or hotels; playing indoor recreational games; walking the dog; attending picnics or barbecues.

Leisure as a challenge

In 1992, the first ever national survey of time use was conducted by the Australian Bureau of Statistics. It showed that the traditional division of labour in the household is changing, if only slowly. The most drastic change was in the kitchen, with a steep decline in women's cooking, especially for women aged in the two groups 33–49 and 55–64. Their average cooking time fell by at least two hours nineteen minutes per week, between 1987 and 1992. The major reasons for this were the popularity of the microwave oven, now in over two-thirds of Australian households, and of convenience foods.

Given this extra time now available to so many Australians, another question to consider is how leisure can be made more desirable. Earlier retirement, retrenchment, technology, electronic expertise, as well as shorter working hours, are forcing this question more dramatically upon Australian society.

The purpose of the United Nations International Day of the Elderly, established in 1991, is to look at the range and diversity of leisure, recreational and cultural opportunities for people aged fifty and over. It provides a focus for the significant achievements and contributions made by older people, and is helping overcome the long-standing myth that older people are incapable of taking active roles in their communities.

In Victoria the day was celebrated in 1995 with up to 10 000 people aged fifty and over enjoying a wide-ranging expo at Caulfield Racecourse. Brisbane City Hall was the venue in Queensland with a day of festivities including ethnic dancing, tap dancing, poetry, music recitals and displays of every kind. The foreshores of Darwin became the focus of Northern Territory celebrations, when members of the Ulysses Club, a dedicated group of motorcycle enthusiasts over forty, invited others to join them. Free pillion rides were offered to those who have forgotten, or wondered, what it is like to feel the wind in their hair.

Another milestone in promoting the pleasures of sporting activity is the Australian Masters Games. The fifth in this series took place in Melbourne in October 1995, to coincide with Victoria's most exhilarating time in sport, the Australian Football League Grand Final and the Spring Racing Carnival. Previously known as the Masters Mile, the Masters Games brought together 10 000 competitors in fifty-three sports for the biggest multi-sports festival ever conducted in Melbourne.

There was everything from archery to woodchopping for people over thirty, in the ten-day event. Beginning with a big welcome celebration at Albert Park, beginners, the moderately and highly competitive and ex-champions took part, always at the level best suited to the individual. All it took was the will to participate. Behind the fun and competition was VicHealth's policy of improving the health of mature-age people, notably in heart health, fitness, weight control, stress reduction and mental wellbeing.

Arts and crafts – a rich repertoire

As the Australia Council has well said, arts and cultural participation can be vital to the mental, physical and emotional wellbeing of people. The Council pointed out, in its submission to the Federal Parliament's Committee for Long Term Strategies, that the arts are now an accepted part of schooling, with about twenty-nine per cent of school students studying creative and performing arts.

Older people who have not enjoyed this attractive aspect of primary and secondary education can and should expect to have more of both with their increased leisure time. Problems of transport, costs and access to events at suitable times are now being addressed by many of those providing artistic and cultural events. Many, for example, are being held in the daytime, and mostly at discounted rates for 'seniors' and 'pensioners'.

> Arts and cultural participation can be vital to the mental, physical and emotional wellbeing of people.

Public libraries, art galleries and museums are the natural reservoirs of materials that can educate and enthral. Concert halls and theatres entertain and inspire. All these places provide a vital social, recreational and educational resource for people of all ages. They do not exist, however, simply as providers of the best this country has to offer; they exist to encourage us to 'have a go'. Whether it is writing, painting, singing, dancing, spinning, carving or any other artistic or craft activity, the work of the creative genius invites us to use our own expressive gifts, no matter how modest they may be. There are innumerable art and craft organisations in every corner of the country; no-one is able to put a figure on the total.

At the more highly skilled level, the Crafts Councils operating in every Australian state and territory aim to enhance the role of professional and aspiring professional craftspeople in our cultural and economic life. Lectures, forums, workshops and specialist publications are part of every Crafts Council agenda. Exhibitions, commissions, consultations, retail and export opportunities are also part of the Council's role.

A data base of Australian craftspeople reveals their extent and expertise. They range from gold- and silversmiths, handknitters, lacemakers, textile designers, potters, spinners and weavers, to embroiderers, quilters, jewellers and metalsmiths, ceramicists and woodworkers. Many have been able to enhance their skill in their later years. One highly skilled wood carver quoted to me the English proverb: 'It is better to begin in the evening than not at all'.

The Australian Bureau of Statistics provides a fascinating insight into the cultural/art/craft interests and activities of our population. The ABS divides cultural and leisure activities into the following areas:

- cultural heritage
- creative and performing arts
- literature
- film and video
- libraries
- radio and television
- sports and recreation
- language
- religious practice
- adult education
- active attachment to custom and place
- activities around conservation and enjoyment of the natural environment.

Performing arts

We all have our favourite performers, actors and artists, and it is astonishing how many of them are fifty-something. Think of people linked with the theatre, actors like Ruth Cracknell, Patricia Kennedy and Jill Perryman, and the playwright Julia Britton. Julia is in the 'upper seventies' and has been quoted as saying she is fed up with condescending ageist articles about the little granny type who amazes people with her advanced years.

She often quotes Bernard Shaw who 'was almost writing on his tombstone'! Julia Britton's latest work, *Perc*, a play based on the life of the Australian composer, Percy Grainger, was enthusiastically researched and written with a mind sharpened by intense interest in the subject.

Then there is the Queensland poet-entertainer Gertrude Skinner, who in her early eighties won the Best Entertainer of the Year award at the Glen Innes Bush Festival, organised by the Returned Services League in 1995. Wife of a shearer and all too aware of the hardship of life on the land, Gertrude always enjoyed making people laugh and now has a huge following in the country and folk music scene. She is also a popular writer, having published two books and three cassettes. She sees a lot of advantages in being old. She can be ruder, she is not worried about money and as long as the arthritis doesn't get to her tongue she will keep writing jokes and yarns, she said in an ABC radio interview.

Visual arts

Betty Churcher has held perhaps the country's most coveted art position, as director of the internationally acclaimed National Gallery of Australia in Canberra. In six years she brought art to the people in new ways, making the gallery less threatening and more welcoming for the great exhibitions staged there. She empowered the public to feel the National Gallery was theirs. During its tenth birthday celebrations more than 1 250 000 people viewed aspects of the gallery's collection outside Canberra. After a lifetime of achievement in the highly competitive art world, her words in a newspaper interview as she contemplated departure, had a heartfelt ring:

> I certainly don't have any worries about the gallery ... It's myself I am so very worried about. What am I going to do? I've been

so busy all my life. I love realising a vision, of seeing a potential and then making it happen. I will miss all that. I walk out the door on 10 January, the day before my sixty-fifth birthday. I really can't bear to think about it, really. Letting go will not be easy.

The fact that Betty Churcher was rumoured by the media in mid-1995 to be on the short list to become Australia's next Governor-General – the first woman to hold the post – speaks much about her potential still, as a woman of enormous capacity. The fact that she did not retire at sixty-five, after all, says much for an enlightened anti-discriminatory policy on the part of the Gallery Trustees.

The water colourist Robert T. Miller lives in a retirement village but spends most of his time out of it, preparing for his next exhibition. Former design director for a large Australian company, he is well into his seventies. The nineteenth solo exhibition of this winner of eighty art awards was held in mid-1995.

Busy hands – quiet mind

There is always, in the creative work of one's hands, no matter how simple, the matter of finding time to be quiet and still. The writer Santha Ramu Rau, in an article entitled 'When the World is Too Much With You', wrote about the need for solitude and reflection:

> Some people find that when their hands are busy their minds are free; for them, the soothing familiar movements of, say, embroidery provide a good framework for private thought.
>
> Whatever device suits you best, the purpose is to enter deeper into yourself than is possible in a normal crowded day, and at the same time to get entirely beyond your own personality into the realms of genuine intellectual, philosophical and spiritual thought.
>
> This refurbishment of the spirit makes it possible to continue as a responsive human being ... and of course the greatest importance of the retreat principle is that it is better for *you*.

> Some people find that when their hands are busy their minds are free.

My mother, in her early seventies, was studying advanced embroidery design in England when she fell and broke her right shoulder, elbow and wrist. The brilliant surgeon who cared for her told her his life's work centred on the human hand, that magnificent instrument that never ceased to fascinate with its endless possibilities for creativity and service. In due course my mother returned home, able once again to do the exquisite embroidery that had been a lifetime passion, and to teach, enthusiastically, until well after her ninetieth birthday.

My own experience of embroidery is that it has always bridged the gap, or rather broken down the rigid separation many people feel between education, work and leisure time. I studied at the Royal School of Needlework in London at nights, often to the derision of my male journalistic colleagues in Fleet Street. Bringing back that training to Australia, and helping found a branch of the Embroiderers Guild in Victoria,* has been perhaps the greatest achievement, and pleasure, of my life. Embroidery is not only taught to the highest standards, but has provided an outlet for thousands of people, mainly but not entirely women, who find pleasure in creating beautiful things.

I had a delightful image of *men* relaxing with a needle in their hands when talking recently to a clergyman retired from a long-term school chaplaincy. When he returned for a reunion, some of the boys asked him what he was doing in his spare time. He replied that among other interests he had taken up 'tapestry', that is canvas work on a frame, and was enjoying the rhythm, discipline and sense of quiet achievement as each piece grew to completion under his hands. To his surprise a number of the boys told him their fathers were doing this too! The fathers were not retired, however; they were professionals and high level businessmen who found some peace and quiet by sitting at an embroidery frame, whenever they could spare the time, an example of all that this book has been espousing.

Parishioners at my local church often noticed the lovely hand-knitted jumpers the vicar, his wife and children wore. It was only on their departure that we learned the knitter was the vicar himself; again he used this as a form of therapy in times of stress, and often ended a hectic day and evening with an hour or so of knitting.

There is also the sense of privacy and the great satisfaction of quiet achievement that countless men derive from time spent on productive leisure in their sheds — but this would fill another book.

Dr Davis McCaughey, a former Governor of Victoria and regarded as one of this country's truly wise men, had some typically thoughtful comments when helping, at the age of eighty, to launch Betty Friedan's book, *The Fountain of Age*, in 1994. This was the book that helped people become 'authentically themselves' with their pains, victories and failures. Dr McCaughey believed the antagonism between the young and the old ought not to be. While the middle-aged could only envisage being successful, the young had hopes for the future and the old were experienced in failure.

Dr McCaughey's concern was how to get rid of the preoccupation with self. He recommended a view of life that went far beyond today's headlines. 'Read one extract from a venerated book like the Scriptures or the classics', he advised. 'The human race did not become wise with this morning's editorial, and ancient wisdom did not die yesterday. The world is much too interesting to be preoccupied with ourselves alone.'

In short ...

1 Say 'Yes' to life.

2 Try to strike a favourable balance between the inner and outer conditions of your life. When this has been achieved, leisure should happen within you.

3 Be prepared to unlearn those negative attitudes to healthy free time that you've developed during your lifetime.

4 Think of moving *to* something in the future rather than retiring *from* something.

5 Consider your life goals, write them down with specific ways of achieving them.

6 List the kinds of satisfaction you are seeking. Think about constructive and realistic ways of achieving them.

7 Compile a personal inventory.

8 Investigate the resources for leisure and recreation vigorously and systematically, based on your leisure inventory.

5
Contributing to a thinking society

'Private life cannot provide all the satisfaction we need — it is unequal to the task.' I do not know who made this perceptive statement, but it encapsulates much of what follows in this chapter.

The value of the volunteer

Professor Ronald Henderson, famous for his report on poverty in Australia, may have sounded well ahead of his time in 1975 when he recommended that ways had to be found to enable old people to contribute something to others, to make use of their experience and abilities, and to develop their skills or to make use of new ones. These phrases form an excellent recipe for volunteerism. They are also in the mainstream of progressive thinking about mature-age people in Australian society today.

They must stay in the mainstream because, by the year 2025, the numbers of people aged sixty-five or over will, for the first time in our history, exceed those aged 0–14 years. The implications of this must be faced, especially by the 'baby boomers' – those born after World War Two – for they and their children will be in the majority category.

I have been warned that 'volunteerism' is an ugly, unpopular word, as is the phrase 'the voluntary sector'. Why not use words like 'citizen or civic friendship', 'community contact' or 'citizen participation'? Someone has said, however, that the idea of 'citizen participation' is a little like eating spinach: no-one is truly against it because it is good for you. Some welfare professionals in fact call the phrase 'the voluntary sector' a 'throwback to the ark'. Well, if other words sit more comfortably in their minds, let them use them.

> Like 'the aged', volunteers have an image problem. They are said to share the low social prestige of the traditional caregiver. But why? Is it because status only comes from high, and highly paid, achievement in business, the professions, sport or politics?

The fact remains that doing something for others gives a sense of completeness that can be found in no other way. The mere act of one individual helping another, we hope, helps the helper in at least four ways:

- the level of interpersonal competence
- a sense of equality in giving and taking between oneself and the other
- the helper learns while helping
- the helper may win social approval.

These factors are especially strong in self-help groups. St Paul's admonition to bear one another's burdens, instructive though it is, is perhaps not the most appropriate here; I prefer his advice to the Colossians: 'Whatever your task, work at it with all your heart'.

Yet, like 'the aged', volunteers have an image problem. They are said to share the low social prestige of the traditional caregiver. But why? Is it because status only comes from high, and highly paid, achievement in business, the professions, sport or politics? If so, then status rests with only a miniscule proportion of our population. Yet if one asks a prestigious organisation like the National Trust of Australia, one is assured they could not survive without the huge army of volunteers who support them.

The 'do-goodism' of Ladies Bountiful that plagued the charities of generations past appears, mercifully, to be disappearing, and in its place is emerging the idea that volunteerism is the social cement of a civilised society. Giving of one's self in any task is not a one-way experience, for the recipient alone. One needs to recognise the needs of the giver. The helper-helped relationship has to be one where mutual trust is paramount.

If we are to give, we need a receiver of course. We need to be needed by others, and until that need is expressed we are not whole persons. It is becoming recognised that the opposite situation, of being not needed, of feeling useless, of not being expected to make a contribution to society, is leaving many young people in communal ghettoes where they can do nothing because they have been trained to do nothing.

> If we are to give, we need a receiver of course. We need to be needed by others, and until that need is expressed we are not whole persons.

Australia has an enormous unpaid labour force in its volunteers. In sport and recreation alone, 3.6 million people provided some 436.4 million hours of voluntary work in Australia in the year up to June 1987 (this figure came from ABS surveys). The ABS acknowledged the difficulty of assigning a market value to these activities, but nevertheless estimated that the labour cost equivalent of the voluntary work in sport and recreation in 1986–87 amounted to $1.7 billion.

Jenni Warburton, a Queenslander working towards a PhD on volunteering by older people, suggests there are about 1.2 million people volunteering through formal Australian organisations, and the government acknowledges that this volunteer labour, even conservatively estimated, is worth billions to the economy.

The Office of Ageing in Queensland made a grant in 1994 to the state's Volunteer Centre (QVC) to pilot a programme, similar to those running successfully in Western Australia and New South Wales, to encourage and support older people in volunteering. QVC, itself with eighty members of its ninety-two staff volunteers, refers about three thousand people each year to community organisations.

Queensland's Retired and Senior Volunteer Programme (RSVP) is based on the belief that the skills and experience of older people are a valuable untapped resource. Wisdom can always be recycled! People over fifty-five are offered positions suited to their background, interests and aspirations. Working in small teams of four to six, volunteers work together on a project combining their skills and providing companionship of peers. The group has a further benefit, in making it possible for a member to have a break for holidays or other reasons, while the rest carry on their chosen task.

There are endless suggestions for volunteering, ranging from helping one's neighbour to serving in another country with Australian Volunteers Abroad.* The essence is to do something that you believe is intrinsically worthwhile. Mature-age people usually have more time to give, and some make volunteer work almost a full-time activity, while others see a few hours each week as satisfying. International Volunteers Day, celebrated in early December, honours this work and also offers opportunities to explore other avenues.

Service clubs like Rotary, Lions, Business and Professional Women, and Zonta retain many people in their retirement years. Municipal Councils and Citizens Advice Bureaus often have a department for volunteer outreach, and welcome enquiries. Religious institutions have enormous numbers of volunteers, and send them out into the community with varied tasks, from driving people for medical treatment and visiting 'shut-ins' to delivering Meals on Wheels and advocacy for the vulnerable and disadvantaged. Volunteers have been called 'the heart and soul' of

Meals on Wheels, which operates with one of the largest voluntary workforces in Australia. Many of those who deliver meals find they are as old, if not older than, those who receive them. They are grateful to be fit enough to combine a pleasurable activity with a sense of purpose.

The Opportunity Shops found all around the country are stocked with goods donated by volunteers for some good cause, while the salespersons too are volunteers. Home tutoring, where one person helps a migrant to learn English, is one of Australia's quiet but great voluntary achievements. Another is the 'talking book' project whereby volunteers record whole novels, textbooks and other printed material for the visually impaired.

Organisations such as the Red Cross, the National Trust, Community Aid Abroad, welfare organisations like the Brotherhood of St Laurence and St Vincent de Paul Society, conservation groups, historical and other cultural societies survive only on the strength of their volunteers. The exciting and productive work done by Project Jonah is done by volunteers irrespective of age. Henrietta Kaye, wife of a well-known Victorian judge, has made the protection of whales and dolphins virtually her life's work since her children became adults. She was awarded the Australia Medal (AM) on Australia Day 1996 for her services to the marine conservation movement, particularly through Project Jonah. Mrs Kaye is proud to claim that Australia is now taking a leading role in the International Whaling Commission.

Many other animal welfare, and specialist breeding associations attract volunteers, who often become expert in the care and habitat of their chosen animal, or bird. There are also the political parties. Local branches of all party persuasions are bewailing the loss of volunteers. So, look around, there is something out there for you!

A Universal Declaration of Volunteering was adopted in Paris in 1990, when the International Association for Volunteer Effort held its 11th biennial conference. It proclaimed its faith in volunteers as a creative and mediating force, notable in three ways:

- in respecting the dignity of all people and their ability to improve their lives and exercise their rights as citizens
- in helping solve social and environmental problems
- in building a more humane and just world, furthering international co-operation.

Such a symbol of solidarity can surely awaken a challenge in every person to be a 'civic friend'. The American writer and naturalist Henry David Thoreau, who had the idea of working for one day a week, and using the rest for the use of his eyes, ears and hands in the Walden woods, wrote the following:

> If you have built castles in the air, your work need not be lost; that is where they should be. Now put the foundations under them.

'Turning thinking into a hobby'

Edward de Bono's memorable phrase, 'Turning thinking into a hobby', should be valued from our early years, so that the habit will continue lifelong.

John Adams, the second President of the United States, wrote this visionary letter to his wife in 1780:

> I must study philosophy and war that my sons may have liberty to study mathematics and philosophy, geography, natural history, naval architecture, navigation, commerce and agriculture, in order to give their children a right to study painting, poetry, music, architecture, statuary, tapestry and porcelain.

Barry Jones, the peripatetic politician who chaired a Commonwealth government inquiry called 'Expectations of Life: Increasing Options for the Twenty-first Century',* used this 'audacious' letter in the findings, which were published in book form in 1992. As Jones wrote, the Industrial Revolution was at its very dawn when Adams penned his letter, horses and water power were the main sources of energy and people toiled on farms to keep themselves alive. 'Two centuries later we have the technological capacity to reduce necessary work to vanishing point, and we can do all the things Adams desired for his grandchildren', Jones states. 'We can transform our society into an activity society. We have very little idea about the potential of which human beings are capable. It is high time we found out.'

Surely a fundamental ingredient in striving to reach our full potential is through education, and in the case of the mature-aged, through returning to learning. It is sad to note how unattractive education can be for secondary school students in particular who are forced to acquire it. Most of us know of 'school refusers', the modern euphemism for adolescents who skip school for other more challenging – and more dangerous – pursuits. Mature-age people with unhappy memories of school can nevertheless find opportunities for learning by seeking out something that really attracts them.

> Surely a fundamental ingredient in striving to reach our full potential is through education, and in the case of the mature-aged, through returning to learning.

The joy of finding an unthreatening environment at a community learning centre, an Adult Education Centre or at a TAFE College, is being expressed daily by enthusiasts who are enrolling in their thousands. In my own municipality the local newspaper advertised no less than 399 classes in its eleven community houses, for one term alone. (This did not include the numerous classes held at commercial art and craft shops, galleries and health centres. One health centre in my area advertises 'massage and health for the over fifties'.) The classes in the community houses ranged from quite simple hobbies to advanced computer courses. These houses are ideal places to begin to regain the competence of earlier years, or indeed to gain a competence one never had.

Learning: a lifelong process

One hears often of mature-aged women at universities whose husbands do not even know they are studying. University lecturers have told me it is acknowledged that women over forty coming into higher education might well find themselves in conflict within their marriage. Tertiary education opens up career possibilities with an intellectual component and unfortunately this can be very threatening to a husband.

Many of these women had no opportunity for further education during their teens, and now, with child rearing behind them, they are free at last to pursue some area of knowledge that not only enriches them, but the family and society as well. Helping husbands understand and support their wives as they blossom academically, intellectually and spiritually is a whole uncharted area. Many people have still to understand that learning is a lifelong process, and is a legitimate activity for everyone, including wives.

> Many people have still to understand that learning is a lifelong process, and is a legitimate activity for everyone.

Women are now outnumbering men at university, and taking over areas traditionally dominated by males. Of all new students entering tertiary study in 1994, fifty-five per cent were women. Most universities provide for the special admission of mature-age people, and some courses are designed for students other than school leavers. It is the fully employed who are most prominent in adult learning, their study obviously related to their career. Personal income is another factor – the poorest and the wealthiest Australians are the least likely to undertake a course. Women are more likely to use an adult education centre than men. Men are most likely to take courses run by employers, unions or industry bodies.

Dynamic seventy-year-olds – and over

Three dynamic seventy-year-olds are proudly promoted by Deakin University as recent graduates. Three very different neighbours living in an elegant retirement village enrolled in of-campus studies. Mrs Beryl 'Ricky' Snowman took up visual arts to complement her already established skills as a landscape painter.

As with her friends, Mrs Gwen Summers and Mrs Lydia Freymuth, it was an opportunity for study not available to her in her younger days.

Gwen Summers was a nurse for most of her working life, and took up politics and international affairs, and since graduating has been researching the achievements of colonial women in Australia. Lydia Freymuth was a twenty-year-old student in her homeland of Estonia when World War Two disrupted her life and she found herself in Australia, in the workforce. She is now a graduate of anthropology. These stories, of mature-age students sharing a love of learning, can be multiplied across every university in the country.

Eileen Stuart gained a Master of Laws degree in 1992 at Monash University at the age of eighty and her thesis, on 'Dissolution and Annulment of Marriage in the Catholic Church', was published by a distinguished law publisher just as she turned eighty-two. Married near the end of the Great Depression in 1933, Eileen and her husband had six children. She found herself reading her son's legal texts to gain some knowledge in matters concerning her husband's business, and enrolled in a mature-age Matriculation course by correspondence. 'I warned my family I would be removing my mind from their affairs, though I was still functioning as usual at the home address', Eileen told me. 'Quite incredibly' she then began studying law, always part-time, at the University of Melbourne. Her memory for new material developed, and in 1978 she was qualified to sign the Victorian Bar Roll. She began practising as a barrister in her late sixties before enrolling in the Master of Laws course to further her interest in family law. Now eighty-four, her fascination with the subject continues, with only one regret, that she did not find it earlier.

College for Seniors

People without the urge for study at this high level have enormous opportunity to do so in less demanding courses. The

Australian College for Seniors,* for example, based at the University of Wollongong, welcomes anyone over fifty years of age, with or without educational qualifications. It has forty participating colleges, universities and adult education organisations, offering programmes that are often linked to educational holidays. A key component is the lecturer, often a university staff member, who has the special skill of not talking down to older people. Participants receiving any type of government pension can apply for a scholarship to undertake one programme, with an automatic payment of $200.

ACFS promotes the 'global classroom' and learning trips to anywhere in the world, as well as in every Australian state, are always on offer. Overcoming loneliness and boredom, raising one's quality of life and disposing of the 'retirement blues' are good reasons for enrolling in ACFS. 'Continuing education can provide new friends and new social groups who can supply the necessary recognition, admiration, feedback and encouragement which people of all ages require', ACFS's founder Barry Russell says. 'Learning keeps people up to date, stimulated and nourished. While you are learning there is less time spent on introspection. It plays an important part in illness prevention.'

> 'While you are learning there is less time spent on introspection. It plays an important part in illness prevention.'

None of this is new, of course. Professionals in the world of 'the ageing' are often heard to quote the wisdom of the Greek philosophers. Plato was reported as saying around the year 400 BC that 'people who engage in intellectual and social activity throughout life will be far better in coping with ageing than those who do not'. Cicero, about 50 BC, wrote that 'decline in ageing can be resisted by physical exercise, a good diet and intellectual activity'.

Open Learning Australia
One cannot over-estimate the value of Open Learning Australia,* which makes university and TAFE education accessible to all, via the Australian Broadcasting Corporation. The word 'open' has

many connotations, in this case of putting control of the process in the hands of the learner, rather than the teacher. OLA operates as an educational broker with government backing, by registering students in new and existing university and training units from more than twenty of our leading institutions. New technologies and teaching methods have made this possible.

Open Learning is all about self-development and fulfilling the desire to improve knowledge and qualifications through formal education, no matter where one lives. Over the past two years more than 12 000 students have registered with OLA. They range in age from an eighty-three-year-old studying towards a Bachelor of Business to a twelve-year-old studying two units in Astronomy.

Twenty units were offered through television and radio programmes in 1995, offering pathways to degrees, diplomas or certificates. All TV programmes, except for languages, are captioned for deaf and hearing-impaired people.

University of the Third Age

Now a worldwide organisation, the University of the Third Age (U3A)* movement began in 1972 in Toulouse, France, to bring older people into contact with academic programmes at the university. It spread rapidly throughout France and Europe, and gained recognition by such bodies as the United Nations and Unesco.

U3A was introduced to Australia in 1984, and is now flourishing in every state and territory. One of its four founders, Cliff Picton, claims this movement is the proudest achievement of his career. 'Participants are open to new ideas, the unfamiliar opens up, and they move from a base of the known and stable to realms of the unknown', Cliff Picton told me. 'U3A encourages people to acknowledge that even the most ordinary lives can have something special. It invites them to open themselves up, to take stock, and then take risks in doing something different.'

> 'U3A encourages people to acknowledge that even the most ordinary lives can have something special.'

Across Australia U3As tap the great reservoir of knowledge, skills and experience to be found among older people and which is often undervalued or overlooked. All of the teaching, planning and administration is carried out by U3A members who value the dignity of exchange, both in knowledge and skill. There is no entry requirement for membership. An essential aspect of every U3A group is members' willingness to teach, as well as to learn. Subscriptions, usually about $25 per year per person or $40 per family, are at a level that does not exclude people dependent upon age benefits or pensions.

Every course is taken at a pace and to a depth consistent with individual ability and personal needs. The social element, in nurturing friendship, is always important. Virtually every U3A group is English speaking, although there have been some sporadic attempts to establish them in other languages. An unusual example of outreach activity was the Geelong (Victoria) branch's introduction of U3A-styled activities in the renal dialysis unit at Geelong Hospital.

Australian U3As, with their 26 000 members, operate with varying emphases. In Western Australia, U3A started at the initiative of University Extension, University of Western Australia. Somewhat different to those in other states, some core lecturers are professional academics who, it is reported, show 'an undisguised delight at the response they receive from an enthusiastic, motivated audience'. Bridging a wide range of ages, U3A in Western Australia takes seriously the original medieval sense of the word 'universitas', a community of scholars.

In Queensland, where already one in every seven citizens is over sixty, U3As are thriving. Of the state's 7000 members, many are concentrated in the south-east corner. Assisted by Griffith University, especially with office space and the use of the library and accounting services, Brisbane's tutors come from the members' own ranks but they are often retired academics still keen to share what they know.

Before leaving the fascinating possibilities offered by U3As, one must pay due deference to Dr Peter Laslett, the English social historian who has made much of the phrase 'The Third Age'. (*Le Troisieme Age* was in use in France in the early seventies.) Laslett describes the whole life course in this idiosyncratic way in his recent book, *A Fresh Map of Life: The Emergence of the Third Age:**

> First comes an era of dependence, socialisation, immaturity and education; second an era of independence, maturity and responsibility, of earning and saving; third an era of personal fulfilment; and fourth an era of final dependence, decrepitude and death.

In this analysis of life experience the divisions between the four ages do not come at birthdays, nor do they even lie within clusters of years surrounding birthdays. Moreover the life career which is divided into these four modules has its culmination in the Third Age, the age of personal achievement and fulfilment, not in the Second Age and emphatically not in the Fourth. It follows logically enough that the ages should not be looked upon exclusively as stretches of years, and the possibility has to be contemplated that the Third Age could be lived simultaneously with the Second Age, or even with the First.

Not everyone would agree with this, of course, for it differs from the description that was in vogue in France in the seventies and in the United Kingdom and Australia in the eighties, 'The Age of Active Retirement'. It is this phrase that has appealed to many, and drawn them into U3A. They recognise what

> In advanced societies today almost every individual has a chance of full experience in the world, 'full in the sense of being in it for as long as they are capable of living'.

Barry Jones sees in the Third Age, the age of greatest freedom, when the pressures imposed by work and family responsibilities have been lifted, but physical and mental health remain good.

Laslett made the point that those in advanced societies today are the first population to exist in which almost every individual has a chance of full experience in the world, 'full in the sense of being in it for as long as they are capable of living'. Before the middle of this century, the greater part of human life potential had previously been wasted by people dying before their allotted time was up.

Short courses for the over-fifties

It is not surprising to find so many mature-age people enrolling in short courses through the Workers Education Association in some states and the Council of Adult Education in Victoria.* Victoria's CAE is said to be unique in the world, with 60 000 students enrolled each year. Its motto is 'You and CAE – partners for life'. Since its inception in 1947, it has forged a place as a comprehensive and lively source of learning for adults. Quality, relevance and joy are its landmarks.

One thousand students studying subjects for the Victorian Certificate of Education range across the state, in preparation for tertiary study. Of 370 students at the CAE's City Centre in Melbourne in 1995, twenty-six per cent were forty-five or older, and thirty-four per cent had left school twenty or more years earlier. Short courses specially targeted at the over-fifty-fives include languages, philosophy, writing, health and fitness, and computers. (There is a fifty per cent discount on every CAE course for any student sixty years or over.)

Leonie Barber, who co-ordinates the Adult VCE Network for rural and community houses and TAFE, states that sixty-three per cent of students rank the 'adult environment' as a major reason for choosing to study through the CAE. Some of the mature-age students have been retrenched. Some have never matriculated, and realise what they have missed, and could now use. Others find study a stabilising experience after illness or sadness. Others are there simply for enrichment, and will continue 'forever', delightedly pursuing some area of knowledge hitherto untapped.

The TAFE sector across Australia is hugely comprehensive. With the increasing demand for vocational education and training and the restructuring of industry, new and different skills are required. The colleges of TAFE, and universities with TAFE divisions, deliver publicly funded and accredited courses in response to the needs of business and industry. Professional training staff deliver courses to well over one million students in the national TAFE sector. Many of these are of mature-age, upgrading existing skills or acquiring new skills.

Adult Learners Week

Australia was involved in the first national Adult Learners Week in September 1995. It proved to be a 'fantastic focus' for new alliances and contacts, with thirty-six (mainly national) organisations joining what is now the ALW National Adult Learning Coalition.

Peter Laslett, adjudged by *The Times* of London to be 'one of the 1000 makers of the twentieth century', was, at the age of seventy-nine, one of many distinguished international official guests. Adhering to his own principles, he spoke in different states about one of his own consuming interests, the navigator Captain James Cook and his family.

> 'Lifelong learning is a basic human right and a universal human value.'

The AWL festival, co-ordinated by the Australian Association of Adult and Community Education, was immensely successful in increasing community awareness of the range and quality of easily accessible adult learning programmes (many of which have been described in this chapter). There were three main themes: Lifelong Learning, Women's Ways of Learning and Leading, and Access for All.

I particularly liked the caption for Lifelong Learning: 'a right, a tool and a joy'. The words of the Director-General of Unesco, Dr Federico Mayor, were used everywhere:

> Lifelong learning is a basic human right and a universal human value; learning and education are ends in themselves, to be aimed at by both individuals and societies and to be promoted and made available throughout the entire lifetime of each individual.

Queensland politician and former educator, Mrs Kathy Sullivan, the Member for Moncrieff, pointed to the voluntary, pleasurable nature of adult learning, with its 'totally motivated clientele', when she spoke in Parliament House Canberra in support of ALW. Even so, she acknowledged the major psychological hurdle women face in stepping out of the home. No matter how supportive husband and children might be in her role as wife and mother, the personal nature of their attitudes may nevertheless leave her with the niggling doubt that she does not have any real effective worth.

It was therefore enticing to read how Viv Ducie, co-ordinator of the Week in Western Australia, is finding herself involved in ever-increasing circles. A chance enrolment in a new Opportunities for Women course at her local TAFE led to a Bachelor of Applied Science degree in 1994 and in her final year she did a project on learning centres. Her report, *Opening Doors*, revealed the benefits of belonging to a learning centre – an experience she herself found more stimulating and relevant than some of the subjects she studied at university. Now she is promoting adult learning across the state.

A patron of Adult Learners Week is Mr Colin Hollis, Federal Member for Throsby in New South Wales. He has called adult learning 'the Cinderella of education', even though around three million Australians participate in some form of further education or training each year. He also regards adult learning as a sleeping beauty, waiting for the prince to come along, hopefully with funding.

Adult learning centres in rural Australia

Adult Education Centres in rural Australia have been helping for over two decades to redress inequities by providing access to learning for country people, especially to those who have been educationally disadvantaged. Most programmes are managed by the local community, which best understands the barriers of distance, time and costs. It is also good to know that distance techniques are opening educational opportunity for increasing numbers of students. Recent figures show that about 60 000 Australians are studying university courses by distance education, and 100 000 are studying TAFE courses the same way.

There is a delightful story about a state-based Country Education Project. Farmers and their spouses were visited during an economic slump, to help build upon the resources they themselves possessed. Upon the claim that they 'couldn't do anything', they were asked what they did during the day and what their interests were. Out came a flood of varied answers. They were musicians, superb cooks, rose gardening experts, authorities on animal husbandry, they knew how to sharpen saws.

People were encouraged to get together in groups, and all these skills and more were used to generate practical education and technological training in disused garages, on farms, backyards and in rooms of farmhouses. Farmers of mature age were passing on skills to thousands of children and young adults in areas where a million-dollar technical school was a faraway dream. It was a project completely owned by rural people who realised that everybody knows something that is valuable. (Rural affairs are dealt with in a later chapter.)

> Farmers of mature age were passing on skills to thousands of children and young adults in areas where a million-dollar technical school was a faraway dream.

Dr Terry Seedsman, an Australian academic specialising in ageing and human development, believes the gift and art of successful ageing are respectively *life* and *effort*. Staying alive requires effort on the part of the older individual to move beyond mere existence, to fields of risk, challenge and adventure, he has stated. An important dimension of adventure is curiosity, the urge to know self as well as the mysteries of life that encompass our physical and social world. Youth does not have the exclusive ownership of risk, challenge and adventure. If they do, Seedsman declares, then it is because older people have relinquished these essential ingredients of a vital existence.

In his book *Ageing is Negotiable*,* he takes the four letters of the word RISK to suggest the elements of healthy risk:

R– develop a *routine* of life that seeks regular refurbishment of self, physically and psychologically

I – *invest* energy and thought in new *ideas* and *interests*

S – establish a *self-styled* sense of direction (goals) by *searching* for *stimulation*

K– build a lifestyle strategy that draws upon the *kaleidoscope* of life options and opportunities.

In short ...

1 Do not expect your private life to provide all the satisfaction you need.

2 Consider the fact that doing something for others, by some form of voluntary work, is a reciprocal enterprise.

3 Don't let any unhappy memories you have of school prevent you from returning to learning. Now the choice is *your own*.

4 Remember that learning is a lifelong process – a legitimate activity for every individual.

5 Intellectual activity allows less time for boredom and introspection. This can go a long way to preventing illness.

6 Learning in a group is socially stimulating, and can overcome loneliness.

7 It is never too late to acquire new skills or to gain or upgrade professional qualifications, even if only for your own satisfaction.

8 Investigate the options available. Consult the list of resources at the back of this book and follow up your desires.

6
Are you keeping well?

It goes without saying that we all want to be well. Wellness is more than the absence of sickness; it is the healthy integration of body, mind and spirit. We have already considered some of the ways in which our mental faculties can be kept alert, so let us now consider how to keep our bodies well.

Good health, that most precious commodity, is to be maintained at all costs, and sometimes the costs are higher as we grow older. Prevention of illness is vital at this time, such as remembering your flu vaccinations. (Hospitalisation rates for the elderly and other high-risk groups jump two- to five-fold during an influenza epidemic.) I have been amazed, since beginning this book, how much information is available to help us stay well. Doctors' and dentists' surgeries, pharmacies, health food stores, hospitals, infant welfare, community health, weight-loss and gym centres all have good information, usually in printed form, there for the asking, or rather for the picking up. So where does one start?

> Wellness is more than the absence of sickness; it is the healthy integration of body, mind and spirit.

Let us begin with eating. By the forties our eating habits are set, and they are difficult to break. Yet it is never too late to change.

Nutrition

The Healthy Diet Pyramid, created by the Australian Nutrition Foundation, should be on the door of every home refrigerator. Its three layers indicate what we should eat least, what we should eat moderately, and what we should eat most. Variety is always important.

The 'eat most' layer, the largest at the bottom of the pyramid, includes bread and cereals, fruit and vegetables, rice, pasta and legumes (these include baked beans, dried beans and peas). They are good sources of energy and nutrients but are low in fats, salt and added sugar.

Anything containing fibre, always a source of vitamins and minerals, fills you up and keeps you regular. One cannot over-emphasise the importance of fibre in one's diet. Known as the 'skeleton' of plants, it remains undigested after eating, helps to prevent constipation and haemorrhoids, contributes to lower cholesterol levels and is an excellent way of dispelling waste.

The more fibre we eat, the more efficiently our bodies work. The World Health Organization in fact has set thirty grams as the minimum fibre requirement per day, and most of us eat less than a third of this amount. A fibre supplement is a sensible way to lift this to the proper total. Your fibre intake is best improved, however, by eating the skins of potatoes, apples and other fruits and vegetables, the outer leaves of lettuce and the fibrous parts of vegetables, such as celery strings, raw or lightly cooked vegetables, wholegrain cereals, breads and brown rice and pulses such as peas, beans and lentils. Vegetables that will increase fibre intake are the cabbage family, broccoli, spinach, brussels sprouts, cauliflower and a coleslaw mixture.

> The more fibre we eat, the more efficiently our bodies work.

Overall, we are encouraged to eat in moderation, each day, lean meat and chicken, low-fat milk, yoghurt and cheese, eggs, fish, seafood, nuts and seeds. These contain protein and other nutrients such as calcium and iron.

For vegetarians, certain nutrients such as protein, iron, zinc and vitamin B12 are depleted when meat is excluded. Anaemia caused by iron deficiency is a nutrition problem for vegetarians, especially women. Egg yolk is therefore advised as a good source of iron. The traditional vegetarian diet is based on milk products, cheese, eggs, cereals, legumes, seeds, nuts, vegetables and fruit. Soy products are important for vegetarians, especially vegans (those who eat neither eggs, meat, nor dairy products). Tofu (bean curd) is a further 'must' for vegans. Vitamin C improves the absorption of plant products, so vegetarians should include Vitamin C-rich foods such as citrus fruits, rockmelon, tomato, capsicum, cabbage and broccoli with the iron-containing family of dried beans, lentils and green vegetables.

Healthy eating can be achieved on a small budget. Variety is still of the utmost importance, but by planning ahead and sticking to your shopping list, by comparing prices and brands, looking for 'specials' and buying in bulk where possible, your purchases will be as valuable as if you had money to burn. There is constant challenge in making the more expensive purchases, such as meat and fish, go further, and it can be done. For example, try jacket potatoes with tasty mince, use grated vegetables and rolled oats in meatloaf, or make your rissoles go further with leftover mashed potato and grated vegetables. Recipes for one or two people, and for people on a budget, are freely available from cookery advisers in gas and electricity organisations, from the Home Economics Associations* in each state, the Australian Nutrition Foundation,* the major food companies, and from the milk, meat, fruit and vegetable industry organisations.

> Healthy eating can be achieved on a small budget.

The kinds of food it is useful to have in store, especially if one lives alone or is preparing for retirement, are those with a long storage life such as frozen vegetables and bread, pastas, breakfast cereals and any canned foods with 'salt reduced' on the label. One should, however, go easy on foods such as cured, canned, corned luncheon meats, salamis, sausages, meat pastes, commercial sauces and many take-away snack foods. These are high in preservatives and in salt content.

Weight control

People becoming less active should eat less, rather than more, food. The Heart Foundation of Australia also recommends that we go easy on alcohol – stick to one or two a day, and keep them small! When eating out, keep a jug of water on the table, and space those drinks.

All advice on diet stresses the necessity to lower our intake of fat, especially the saturated fat found mainly in animal foods and dairy products. A low fat diet helps to keep both blood cholesterol and weight down. Cholesterol is a fatty substance made mainly by the liver and our bodies need it in small amounts, but too much in the blood causes the artery-blocking process behind heart disease. The Heart Foundation recommends that all adults know their cholesterol level. Overweight people tend to have higher blood cholesterol levels as well as higher blood pressure levels.

> A low fat diet helps to keep both blood cholesterol and weight down.

Low fat dairy products should therefore be the choice, along with the fruit, vegetables and cereals mentioned earlier in this chapter. Fat should be removed from meat, fresh or tinned fish should be taken two or three times a week, and food should be steamed or grilled, rather than fried or baked in oil. Cakes, pastry, creamy soups and sauces, biscuits and snack foods should be cut down drastically. Nuts, avocadoes and cheese have a high fat content, but in small quantities have a place in a balanced diet.

Being overweight is a cancer risk as well as a heart risk. Keeping to a healthy weight is of course more easily said than done for the majority of middle-aged Australians. The Heart Foundation's weight-loss guide is easily accessible, and costs nothing.* The Foundation's tick of approval on many foods on supermarket shelves indicates they have been independently tested to meet its guidelines on fat, salt, sugar, cholesterol and fibre. The Foundation also publishes a sensible and appealing recipe book.

Fad or crash diets just do not work. On the other hand, it would be wrong to dismiss those weight-loss centres that provide a good service, where counsellors are tactful and interested, and whose results can delight those prepared to follow and stay on a sensible regime. Appetite suppressants should be avoided.

Market influences for the future point directly to those people aged 45–54, and those over seventy-five, as the groups who will be part of Australia's greatest growth over the next five years. Research commissioned by the Conference of Australian Milk Authorities shows that consumers see milk as convenient, good for you, good tasting, satisfying, energy giving, refreshing and delicious. It has been described as a 'cocktail' of nutrients. Milk is not only a valuable source of high quality protein and energy, but, in three glasses per day it provides a high proportion of the requirements of vitamins A, B1 and B2, and the calcium necessary for healthy bones and teeth at every age. Low fat milk is calcium enriched, and therefore especially beneficial for the over-fifties. Buttermilk, and buttermilk-skim also have higher levels of calcium – and lower levels of fat – than regular full-cream or long-life milks.

Calcium intake

The importance of calcium in building healthy bones is especially crucial for people from their mid-thirties on, when bones gradually start to lose calcium. Recent findings show that over seventy per cent of women and fifty per cent of men lack vital calcium levels in their diet. Adults should therefore try to have at least one serve of calcium-rich food with each meal. Older women need more, so calcium-enriched, low-fat dairy foods are an ideal alternative to regular products.

Osteoporosis, a condition where calcium is lost from the bones, which become thin and brittle and liable to break more easily, is more common among women than men. Although this condition is rarely seen in men before sixty years of age, it is likely to become more common as the male life expectancy increases.

The incidence of hip fractures exceeds that of cancer of the breast, cervix and uterus combined. Three thousand women sustain a hip fracture each year with fifty per cent who were able to walk prior to the injury unable to walk afterwards and in need of long-term nursing care. Twenty per cent of these women will die within twelve months due to complications.

> It is important that women maintain an adequate supply of calcium, no matter what their age.

Up to the mid-thirties, women's bones are laying down calcium. After the menopause, the process reverses. If women do not reach this crucial turning point in good shape there is a risk they will develop osteoporosis. Their decreased oestrogen production at menopause, in addition to a very low intake of calcium throughout their younger years are important factors in bone loss. It is important that women maintain an adequate supply of calcium, no matter what their age.

Post-menopausal women can now be prescribed low-dose hormone replacement therapy; as well as other benefits, HRT has been found to be effective in reducing or stopping calcium mineral loss. This is of immense importance, since calcium mineral cannot be readily replaced once it is gone; it is therefore vital to detect osteoporosis in its early stages to try to stop or slow the rate of calcium mineral loss. The earlier women have a test to measure their bone mineral density, the better. The test is a simple one, but done on a specific machine set up in certain radiology centres around Australia. Your doctor will advise on where these are situated.

> The earlier women have a test to measure their bone mineral density, the better.

Osteoporosis is best prevented by lifestyle modifications. One should take regular exercise, maintain weight within a healthy range, and refrain from smoking. Since calcium intake is an important factor, it is essential to consider what foods provide this mineral, and include them in one's diet. While dairy products are among the richest sources of calcium, they are also high in fat content, so it is wise to select the low-fat types of these products. Canned fish such as sardines and salmon, eaten with the bones, is rich in calcium. Fortified soy milk has the same calcium content as the equivalent amount of cow's milk, and tahini (sesame paste) is another useful source.

Let us, however, conclude this section on healthy eating by suggesting some simple hints for making light, easy-to-digest meals for jaded appetites. For those who eat little, judiciously adding dairy foods to cooking will improve their nutritional value:

- Add milk powder or grated cheese (low-fat) to mashed potato (indeed add skim milk powder to dishes during preparation of dishes such as stews and casseroles, as an easy way to boost the family's calcium intake, without their noticing).
- Add grated low-fat cheese to scrambled egg.
- Serve vegetables with a cheese sauce.
- Add an extra slice of cheese to sandwiches.
- For dessert, try jelly whips, junkets, custards and other milk puddings.
- Yoghurt can be used as an excellent low-fat salad dressing, and is delicious with savoury flavourings like mint or garlic.
- Have low-fat, calcium-enriched milk drinks between meals, hot with a sprinkle of nutmeg, hot chocolate, iced coffee, milkshakes or smoothies made with yoghurt.

Let's take heart

Heart disease is the leading cause of death in Australia. Each year it is responsible for almost half of all deaths in this country. Approximately 55 000 people die each year from cardiovascular disease. Much of it is preventable. The main culprits are tobacco, high blood pressure and raised blood cholesterol levels. (These three are the same risk factors in regard to stroke.) Combined risk factors not only add to, but multiply the risk. A person with all three major risk factors is ten times more likely to suffer heart disease than his or her normal counterpart. Risk is reduced by eating a healthy diet, enjoying regular exercise and not smoking. If you belong to a family with a history of heart disease, there is every reason to pay attention to the avoidable risks.

> Heart disease is the leading cause of death in Australia. Much of it is preventable.

Heart disease, caused by the artery-clogging process which starts early in life, is not basically a man's disease. Heart and blood vessel disease is the number one killer of Australian women. While few women suffer from these before menopause, after the age of fifty they do so at an increasing rate. By the time they are sixty, more women die from heart and blood disease than from breast cancer, and many more after that age. The fact that heart disease tends to strike women later than men does not mean women should put off doing anything about it until middle age.

The following five questions will give you an idea of whether you are on the right track for a healthy heart:

- Are you a non-smoker?   Yes/No
- Is your blood pressure OK?   Yes/No
- Is your cholesterol level low enough?   Yes/No
- Are you a healthy weight?   Yes/No
- Do you get regular exercise?   Yes/No

If all your answers are Yes, you are well on the way. The more Nos you have, the greater your risk of heart disease. If you don't know the answers to some of the questions, find out now!

Active at any age

All health literature speaks of the need for exercise. Because only one-third of the people in Victoria were doing any kind of regular physical activity, the programme 'Active at Any Age'* was established in 1990. Sponsored by the Victorian Health Promotion Foundation, the 'Disuse Syndrome' was tackled head on. The programme is especially important for Victoria, which expects to have more older persons than the overall national estimates by the year 2031. The Bureau of Statistics predicts that 27.6 per cent, or 1 608 000 Victorians will be sixty years or over by that date. The programme's target was the older person who had not engaged in physical activity over a protracted period of time, the person reflecting obesity, depression, accelerated ageing, fragile bones and vulnerability to heart disease. Many in this group have responded to the negative message 'act your age', as if it meant one had to slow down, and take it easy. The 'well-earned rest' could too easily sink into apathy. Yet most Victorians, like people all around Australia over fifty-five, are well-aged, with only a minority experiencing poor health, poverty or isolation.

> All health literature speaks of the need for exercise.

At the heart of 'Active at Any Age' is the hope that mature persons will enjoy prolonged vitality, that they will remain physically, psychologically and socially robust, healthily and enthusiastically involved in pursuing life to the fullest. With vigorous promotion on 182 billboards and 10 000 brochures printed in thirteen different languages, the 'Active' office operating out of the Department of Sport and Recreation is now receiving at least 125 enquiries each month.

> An easy walk for a few kilometres is probably just as good as a run over the same distance. It is the total energy you use over a week that counts.

The Heart Foundation confidently asserts you do not have to do vigorous exercise to be heart healthy. Aerobic exercise, that is doing something that makes you puff and sweat for twenty to forty minutes two or three times a week, can be good. You can, however, get similar benefit from milder activity. An easy walk for a few kilometres is probably just as good as a run over the same distance. Leisurely swimming, cycling, tennis or golf is good, for it is the total energy you use over a week that counts. You should always be able to talk or whistle during exercise; that is why laughing or chatting with a friend whilst exercising makes it all the more enjoyable.

If moderation is your choice, it is important to be active on most days. If even this is too hard to begin with, try every second day, to give muscles and joints a rest in between. Listen to your body and make sure you are comfortable at all times. For readers of this book, the Heart Foundation again is reassuring. It is not too late to take up exercise in middle-age or older. Taking up physical activity in later years will still give protection against heart disease, even if you did little exercise when young. There is of course no absolute guarantee against heart disease, but surely anything that can reduce cholesterol levels and help lower blood pressure is worth trying.

Here are the Heart Foundation's simple suggestions to help make exercise a part of everyone's day:

- Take the stairs instead of the lift.
- Walk an extra bus stop before work.
- 'Sign up' for lunchtime activities at work.
- Do exercise you will enjoy and want to do regularly.
- Always start at a low level and if you want to exercise harder, build up slowly over the weeks.
- Don't overdo it; if you do, you could become exhausted, injure yourself and even lose interest.
- Choose shoes with soft or shock-absorbing soles and clothes to suit the weather and type of exercise.
- Don't drive when you can walk easily.

If you have been inactive and want to begin at a more vigorous level, consult your doctor first. You should avoid exercise if the weather is extremely hot, humid or cold, if you have illness such as a cold, or if you have just eaten or taken alcohol.

An enticing list prepared by Victoria's Cancer and Heart Offensive, of 'twenty-five ways to be active for life' is worthwhile for everyone. Some have already been quoted in other contexts, but they are repeated if you are willing to give thirty minutes a day to an activity you enjoy and that suits your age. Here they are:

- Walk with a friend or family. You will enjoy the company, and you're more likely to stick to it.
- Walk the dog every day. The dog will appreciate this too.
- Instead of driving to the shop or work, leave a little earlier and walk.
- Walk to lunch, or pack your own lunch and eat it in the park.
- The beach is always full of life. Take a romantic stroll at dusk.
- Walk an extra bus or train stop. Increase the distance, one stop at a time.
- Take the stairs instead of the lift. You don't have to overdo it. Just one floor can get the heart pumping.
- Discover your city on an organised walking tour.
- Gardening is a surprisingly relaxing way to keep fit.
- Take the grandkids to the zoo, the park, or become involved in their sports as trainer, goal umpire or coach.
- Bicycle riding allows you to see as much or as little of the environment as you like.
- Explore the beauty of gardens open to the public.
- Explore the scenic walking tracks of which your local council has a list.
- An hour or two's shopping in a busy market or department store is wonderful for fitness. Window shopping costs nothing.
- Tennis clubs often have a day of the week dedicated to senior competitions and are always looking for new members.
- Take up lawn bowls. You're never too old or too young.
- Housework can become part of your daily exercise regime. Washing up, hanging out the clothes, vacuuming, and washing the windows can add up to vigorous workout.
- You don't have to be superfit to join a gym. Choose the gym that's right for you.

- Swimming or even just wading in the water can increase your heart rate. Ask your local pool manager about water aerobics.
- In Europe people go for a 'paeso' (little walk) after dinner. It helps digestion and provides a good time for couples or families to be together.
- Sign up for lunchtime or after-work activities.
- Galleries and museums increase your walking while offering an appreciation of arts and culture.
- Bushwalking trails appeal to the more adventurous.
- Waterways are waiting to be explored.
- Golf can increase your walking, and lower that handicap.

Remember, all of the above can be beneficial if done briskly so that you are aware of your breathing, but still comfortable.

Keeping up appearances

As well as feeling good, we all want to look good. Appearances do matter. They tell a lot. If a face lift or a tummy tuck will make a difference to how we feel about ourselves, why not have it? More importantly, our vitality, energy and mobility are all tied up with our appearance, how we feel about ourselves and how we appear to others.

If we were to value elderly people at a societal level, through the media and particularly through advertising, we would more likely see such people being more expressive about themselves. For example, we do not see very many elderly people wearing bathers, enjoying sun, sand and beach, or even walking in that environment. Too many of our messages invite them to 'cover up', because society says they do not look good. This of course has an impact on how they are treated. As David Suzuki advises, we need to respect the wisdom of our elders — and the way they look. Integration rather than segregation is needed by all of us.

The language of clothing is one in which we all have a voice, for we make a statement when we put on our clothes. We all make judgements about others according to their clothes: they can, at an instant, be dubbed patrician, authoritative, feminine, creative, under-stated, businesslike, glamorous, shabby, careless, or easy-going. Grooming, how we keep our hair, make-up for women, shaving for men, all these relate to outward-inward congruence and balance. The use of colour is a further expression of the self. 'Power dressing' seems an unfortunate phrase for the kind of clothes some career women wear. Yet it *can* say 'I count' in an environment where women are competing with others, women or men.

> We need to respect the wisdom of our elders – and the way they look. Integration rather than segregation is needed by all of us.

The body itself has a real bearing on how we look. There are very few of us with perfect bodies. The old-fashioned 'gym' has lost its attraction in the craze for more glamorous, multi-functional services offered at variously named exercise centres. For those of us who do not indulge in the new high art of body maintenance offered at these centres, it is reassuring to know that the eye can always be drawn away from our body's bad spots. As one designer told me, 'Your bad spots are nobody else's business'.

> Your bad spots are nobody else's business.

If one's feet are not good, a regular visit to the podiatrist is more helpful, and a greater boost to morale, than a visit to the hairdresser. Looking after one's feet is, in fact, essential to good posture as well as to good health. It is amazing how often sore or tired feet – a common problem for women who choose their shoes for fashion or vanity rather than for comfort – show in the face.

Let us not forget the importance, indeed the beauty of strong and healthy teeth. Remember the ditty of that humorous English poet, Pam Ayres, 'If only I'd looked after me teeth'? Tooth decay continues to occur throughout life, so there is no escaping the rule we thrust upon our children: 'Don't forget to clean your teeth'. The best news is that with proper care, most of us, unlike earlier generations, can expect to keep our teeth all our lives. The simple basics are daily brushing and flossing, and regular visits (at least twice yearly) to the dentist.

To avoid the build-up of plaque it is important to clean teeth – and gums – at least twice a day. Each tooth has five surfaces, a front, back, two sides and a top. To prevent dental disease, the only sure way is to clean every one of these surfaces. Your dentist will advise if you need a special toothbrushing technique.

Flossing is imperative for removing the debris that builds up between the teeth and under the gumline and cannot be removed by the toothbrush. Sometimes a teflon dental ribbon is easier to use in a mouth crowded with teeth. It is a good idea to carry a packet of tooth picks in one's car or bag.

Sensitive teeth and gums – notably reacting to both hot and cold foods or drinks – often occur in mature-aged people. They are an early warning sign of more serious dental problems. Over time, the protective enamel that naturally insulates the teeth can wear down, especially if the toothbrush used has been too hard, or if the brush has not been used correctly.

Incorrect brushing can also lead to gum recession, leaving exposed the more sensitive roots of the teeth. This is the basis of that well-known expression ascribed to older people 'getting long in the tooth'. The dentist may prescribe one of the sensitive-care toothpastes made for these cases, or fluoride treatment, in any case only a professional can advise how the teeth can be insulated against pain. A word of warning: beware of the whiteners you see advertised. Ask your dentist before deciding which, if any, of the products is worthwhile.

Caring for the carers

An almost invisible group is the army of carers in our community. How they themselves feel, and indeed how they are, is frequently brushed aside, in the interests of the person or persons they care for. The carer can be caught in the sandwich between caring for an elderly parent, and growing or grown children. She or he carries more than the fair share of responsibility, especially in the families of non-English speaking background, in Aboriginal and Torres Strait Islander families, and in families where there is a permanent disability.

> The carer can be caught in the sandwich between caring for an elderly parent, and growing or grown children.

A woman friend, having finished caring for late teen-age children and begun to enjoy a new sense of freedom, then acquired a new house guest: a very frail mother. She said to me sadly: 'The hardest part is that I am now doing things for Mum that she once did for me'.

People over fifty provide the bulk of aged care in Australia, both within their own families and as volunteers in community groups. At present there is one elderly person in six per cent of households, and this is expected to rise to ten percent within fifty years. A survey by the Australian Bureau of Statistics in 1988 showed that fifty-five per cent of persons over sixty years living at home expressed some need of help. The figure was higher if in the family there was someone with a continuous disability. The ABS survey of 1993 showed that women are three times more likely to be carers than men, and women predominate in the carer role up to the age of seventy. Family help is nevertheless declining, as families become smaller. The spinster daughter of other generations, who gave her life to looking after home and parents, seems to have disappeared into the workforce, into her own unit, or into a 'relationship'.

It is not surprising that elderly parents should want independence, as do their offspring, while both want to maintain contact, and often some kind of reciprocal service. No-one underestimates the value of care given by the older generation in terms of baby minding, shopping, or help with household cleaning and gardening to younger families. One often hears the question: 'Just who is dependent upon whom?'

Time-out from caring is expressed as the greatest need for carers, no matter what the circumstances. Because carers are so often denied the opportunity for socialising, or recreation, some special projects have been introduced. In Victoria, there is a Project for Older Women and Women Carers and one of its main tasks is to identify the barriers to – and strategies for increasing – participation in recreation. As the Carers Associations* in every state have shown, carers are as different as the people they care for; 'carers are just ordinary people who have responded compassionately to immediate and often very desperate needs'. They are single parents caring for children with physical or intellectual disabilities, friends looking after loved ones with terminal illnesses, adult children caring for elderly parents who are frail or who have dementia, spouses looking after partners who have had a serious accident, relatives caring for those with mental illness.

> Time-out from caring is expressed as the greatest need for carers, no matter what the circumstances.

They must not be allowed to battle on alone. They need supportive friends with whom they can share their feelings of guilt, anxiety, and physical and emotional inadequacy. They need advice when the person cared for becomes manipulative and manoeuvres the carer into a deeper sense of obligation than is warranted.

They should also seek out the carer support kits, available through Carers Associations in many community languages. Apart from advice on carers' legal rights and financial entitlements, the kits have information on safety around the home, respite and counselling services. One can also ask for specific advice on such problems as ageing, AIDS, arthritis, cerebral palsy, diabetes, emphysema, head injury, incontinence, multiple sclerosis, muscular dystrophy, Parkinson's disease, stroke and many others.

Full-time carers on the Department of Social Security's Carer Pension need to keep themselves informed on their entitlements. A carer can have up to forty-two days in a calendar year to rest, to have a holiday and even to travel overseas, and still continue to be paid the Carer Pension. In addition, a carer can take off up to ten hours a week to work, study or receive training. Social Security advisers can help with work, with training or with child care under the JET (Jobs, Education and Training) scheme.

In 1994–95 the Federal Government allocated $893 000 for age-care support throughout country areas. Carers in country Australia have been particularly vulnerable, and have indicated their greatest need is 'time out'. Women carers are again in the majority, and, as expected in our rural culture, strive hard to meet community expectations by being fully responsible in providing care for family members, often without help from others. Stress naturally follows, with painful back, arthritis and heart disease being common outcomes. One can easily imagine why two Americans, Mace and Rabins, have called their book for those looking after dementing persons *The 36 Hour Day*.

Getting on top of it

Depression is the everyday term for people feeling sadness or grief, but is also a clinical term for a form of mental illness. We need to differentiate between sadness and depressive illness. Reactive depression often occurs after a death or some

> We need to differentiate between sadness and depressive illness.

kind of serious failure, but it usually disappears in time. If not, the depressed person should seek professional help. Epidemiological studies, for example, are showing that divorce and separation are strongly linked to a broad spectrum of mental health problems. Single parents, most of whom are divorced or separated, constitute a particularly vulnerable group.

This twentieth century has been called 'the age of anxiety'. Stress may be a normal part of life, but it can be exacerbated by any number of causes. These include sickness in the family, loss of a friend, financial concerns, excessive strain at work. Life stresses range from mild worry to attacks of panic. Common problems are tiredness, fatigue, sleep disturbance, poor concentration, restlessness and irritability. Stress becomes a problem when you are unable to deal with it, and prolonged or accumulated stress can show in a variety of illnesses. These include depression, irritable digestive system, irritable bladder, peptic and mouth ulcers, impotence, headache, dizzy turns, rapid pulse, dermatitis, heart disease, breast pain and cancer.

> The best way to manage stress is to change your lifestyle. Relaxing takes learning.

When people say they are having a cigarette or an alcoholic drink 'to relax', the physical effects are probably adding to stress by raising blood pressure. Tranquillisers are usually nothing more than a short-term solution.

The New South Wales Health Department has produced a helpful brochure, *How to Relax and Reduce Stress*.* Basically, it shows that the best way to manage stress is to change your lifestyle. It lists useful ways of looking at stressful situations:

- Remind yourself that a physical or mental stress is only a strain when you are not handling it properly.
- The best thing to do is learn how to deal with problems so that they don't upset you too much.
- Don't make mountains out of molehills.
- Try to avoid stressful situations ... get up earlier to avoid the rush, organise things at work, try to avoid annoying activities and people.
- Don't try to do everything at once.
- Talk to someone about your bad feelings ... talking about a problem is often the first step in solving it.
- Live in the present.
- Learn to relax!

Relaxing takes learning. Try the following, suggested in the brochure mentioned above:

> Sit in a comfortable chair or lie on your back on the floor with your head and knees supported by pillows. Loosen any tight clothing. Breathe slowly and regularly for a few moments, saying

the word 'relax' to yourself each time you breathe out. Now think about different parts of your body, allowing each part to relax as you continue to breathe regularly and say the word 'relax'. Some people find it helpful first to tense up the part of the body on which they are concentrating, then let go the tension and focus again on their breathing while all the tension drains away. Start with your toes and work upwards; calf muscles, thighs, abdomen, fingers, forearms, upper arms, small of the back, back of the neck and shoulders and finally, the little muscles around eyes and brow.

If you have trouble relaxing parts of your body, it often helps to get someone else to massage the area gently while you think about relaxing it. When not saying the word 'relax' to yourself it is best to keep your mind on tranquil thoughts as far removed as possible from your daily life.

An even simpler and frequently effective method, the relaxation response, consists of quietly breathing with the eyes either closed or fixed on your hand or thumb. Let any thoughts float through your mind or away. Don't try to hold them. With each outward breath say 'one' or 'relax' softly. Continue to do this. If you have religious beliefs you may wish to use the name of a religious symbol or deity instead.

The more often you relax, the more easily you can do it. Try to set aside a regular time once or twice each day for about ten to twenty minutes' relaxation. Yoga, transcendental meditation and biofeedback techniques help some people. You can also seek advice from local health workers about cassette tapes on relaxation to suit you. You will have to find out, possibly by trial and error, what works best for you.

Professor Gavin Andrews, Professor of Psychiatry at the University of New South Wales, and head of the Anxiety Disorders Clinic at St Vincent's Hospital Sydney, has reassuring comments about stress for people in middle age or older. 'Stress means that bad things are happening to you, but the older you get the better you survive standard stress.'

Two things happen when stress befalls older people, he explains. First, they have more experience, so that they can do something to resolve the thing that appeared at the age of eighteen to be the end of the world. Second, the older one gets the less sensitive one becomes to threat. 'This means the older people are, the better is their mental health', Professor Andrews adds. 'They are less anxious, there are fewer new cases of depression, and alcohol and drug abuse. The older you get, the wiser you get, and you don't necessarily get sadder. It is fantasy to suggest that old people need valium.'

> The older you get, the wiser you get. It is fantasy to suggest that old people need valium.

Dr Tony Jorm, of the Social Psychiatry Research Unit at the Australian National University, states that one of the most neglected aspects of old age is the good news, based on epidemiological community surveys, that people are less likely to become depressed as they become older. Physical health is the biggest risk factor; it is therefore natural that the onset of a physical disability among ageing people may lead to depression.

Professor Scott Henderson, psychiatrist and Director of ANU's Social Psychiatry Research Unit, also points to the 'interesting possibility' that depressive disorders are lower in older than in younger adults. This is one of the benefits that later life can bring.

A good night's sleep

To stay well there is also the question of sleep. Not all of us are blessed with the sleep of angels and no-one is truly well without a good night's sleep. Dr David Morawetz offers what he calls an effective and clinically proven alternative for the two million Australians who say that they regularly have trouble sleeping. Dr Morawetz has had a sleep problem himself, exacerbated by intense study and preparation for his thesis on the topic of sleep! He

> Not all of us are blessed with the sleep of angels and no-one is truly well without a good night's sleep.

tested 159 people around Australia, and has since produced *Sleep Better Without Drugs*.* This is a 4–6 week self-help programme, with fifty things you can do to help yourself to sleep better. You find the solutions that work for you.

David Morawetz states that he has had an eighty per cent success rate with previously poor sleepers. Medication is useful if used not more than once or twice a week, but when it is used every night for long periods, it can become addictive. 'Falling asleep is a bit like surfing', he told me. 'You have to learn to catch the wave, in this case the wave of sleepiness. The natural sleepiness cycle is about 60–90 minutes.' He warns that if you read in order to get to sleep, you should put down the book as the wave comes over you; trying to struggle to the end of the chapter can cause you to miss the wave of sleep.

Therapeutic massage

This may be an appropriate place to refer to people's hunger for human touch. Psychologists call it 'touch deprivation'. It seems to accompany advancing years for many people, as their circle of intimacy decreases. The advantages, both physically and psychologically, of therapeutic massage, are real. Especially if one lives alone, massage by a sympathetic masseur is a beautiful way to reduce stress, and to nourish the self.

> 'Touch deprivation' seems to accompany advancing years for many people, as their circle of intimacy decreases.

If, on the other hand, the luxury of a private massage is beyond your means, you might think of searching out a massage group, perhaps through your local gym. Or you may have a trusted friend with whom the gentle touch can be reciprocated. Some older people take turns to massage each others' feet, and find the experience not only soothing to toes, soles and heels but a relief from headaches and general weariness.

Massage of the face, neck and shoulders is equally soothing, and is delightful when shared by partners. The use of vegetable oils to help the hand slide easily over the skin is recommended. Aromatherapists suggest that one should seek advice from a practitioner, and ensure the botanical name is on the label of an essential oil, to ensure the contents are pure plant extract, and not simply perfumed. Only a few drops in the carrier (vegetable) oil are necessary.

Among the special aromatic oils available, men appear to prefer cedarwood, recommended to reduce anxiety, or basil, for study and clear thinking. Lavender oil is perhaps the biggest seller for relaxation. Other popular oils are frankincense and sandalwood for stress relief, myrrh for meditation, lemon for refreshment, camomile for insomnia, peppermint for muscle aches and pains, mandarin for depression and tea-tree as an antiseptic.

Substance abuse

One could not address any consideration of wellness without facing the problems of nicotine, alcohol and proprietary drug abuse. The latest statistics from the Commonwealth Department of Human Services and Health provide an overview of the harm caused by both legal and illegal drugs in the Australian community. 'Drug-caused' harm, according to the National Drug Strategy, may take the form of illness, disability, social dysfunction, and ultimately death. The publication *Statistics on Drug Abuse in Australia 1994* shows there were 123 660 deaths in Australia in 1992. An estimated 26 355, or about one in every five, of these deaths was caused by drug use amongst all age groups. These statistics on death do not and cannot quantify the pain and suffering of both users and the families of users.

> 'Drug-caused' harm may take the form of illness, disability, social dysfunction, and ultimately death.

Tobacco is the major source of drug-related mortality in Australia, despite the fact that Australian Bureau of Statistics figures show smoking has dropped by one quarter since the late 1970s. This drop has been due mainly to an acknowledgement of the health problems associated with smoking, and the active discouragement – often to the point of total restriction – of smoking by public authorities and major companies.

Tobacco is also responsible for the majority of drug deaths in persons over thirty-five. The number of Australian deaths from tobacco use in 1992 (in the form of cancer, heart disease, chronic bronchitis and the like) in the 35–64 age group was 4761, in the over sixty-five age group 13 977. Although concern is continually expressed about the take-up rate of smoking among young women, the outlook for older women is not all that positive. The National Drug Strategy's household survey in 1993 found that eleven per cent of female respondents over fifty-five were smoking an average of eighteen cigarettes a day, while seventeen per cent of males over fifty-five were smoking an average of sixteen cigarettes per day.

> The lungs are not the only victims, for smoking also contributes to cancers of the lips, mouth, throat, gullet, kidney, pancreas and cervix.

QUIT research has identified smokers over fifty years as the group least likely to accept the health risks of smoking, yet even a reduction in heavy smoking in this age group could greatly reduce heart disease and death. QUIT produced a new promotional booklet, *Now's the Time to Stop: Help for Older Smokers*,* and the launch coincided with Veterans and Senior Citizens Week. The pleasing result: 3000 calls from the over-fifties age group within the first two weeks.

The lungs are not the only victims, for smoking also contributes to cancers of the lips, mouth, throat, gullet, kidney, pancreas and cervix. It has been found that those who have tried to stop, and started again, often succeed the second or third time around. In brief, the successful quitter will:

- want to stop
- be confident there is good reason to stop
- decide to stop and set a date
- stop completely

- avoid situations where temptation is at hand
- understand it is normal to crave a cigarette occasionally and know this will fade in time
- avoid alcohol for the first few days
- avoid putting on weight by exercise and three *healthy* meals each day
- keep trying!

If you are among those trying to cope with that craving, QUIT offers the four 'Ds'. DELAY – for at least five minutes; DRINK WATER – sip it slowly; DEEP BREATHE – slowly and deeply; and DO SOMETHING ELSE – keep your hands busy. Remember too that the withdrawal symptoms when you quit, like coughing, headaches and upset digestion, are good news. You are going through what is called a 'healing crisis'. These symptoms show you that your body is flushing out the chemicals from the tobacco and readjusting. And they won't last long. Nor will the depression, tension, forgetfulness or curiosity about 'just one little cigarette' last more than a few weeks. For older quitters, the most dramatic improvement is in the circulation, the flood of blood through your body.

Talking to others who have quit smoking, or who are trying to do so, about any shared problem is usually of mutual assistance, for only those who have been in the same predicament can truly recognise the other's vulnerability.

Alcohol is second only to tobacco as the major source of mortality in Australia. Alcohol consumption, too, has been falling since the mid-1970s. Drinkers over fifty-five have, however, had the highest levels of daily drinking, according to the National Drug Strategy's household survey in 1993. Deaths in 1992 caused by alcohol (through cancer, alcoholism, alcoholic liver cirrhosis and road injuries) for the 35–64 age group numbered 2184. For those in the over sixty-five age group the number was 3531.

In contrast, the number of deaths in 1992 due to other drugs such as opiates and barbiturates was 277 for the 35–64 age group, and sixty-four for those over sixty-five. Deaths due to illicit drugs in the age group over thirty-five was only one per cent of drug-related deaths.

Alcoholism is a major mental and physical health issue among Australian men, who, according to the National Health and Medical Research Council (NHMRC), are at higher risk of developing the disorder and experiencing its adverse consequences because of their greater exposure to heavy drinking.

The links between alcohol abuse and social disruption are also well documented. Issues like domestic violence, family breakdown, child abuse and incest are all the subject of much research.

There is no absolutely safe level of alcohol consumption. The NHMRC defines low risk drinking as four-standard drinks a day for men, and two for women, *with at least two alcohol-free days each week*. Do not top up unfinished glasses! Anything over four drinks a day for women and six drinks for men is described as harmful. One should not drink at all while taking other drugs or medicines, and certainly if one intends to use machinery. Remember too, it is illegal to drive if your blood alcohol level exceeds 0.05 grams per 100 millilitres.

> There is no absolutely safe level of alcohol consumption.

The risks associated with harmful and hazardous drinking include damage to the brain, liver, intestines, pancreas, muscles, heart, stomach and nervous system. In its educational role, the NHMRC sinks a few myths about alcohol. For example, you must not believe any of the following:

- It's OK to save up all your drinking for the weekend.
- Coffee, cold showers and getting some fresh air can sober you up.
- Alcohol only affects your health when you are old.
- Alcohol helps you to sleep.

Don't worry – it may never happen

Middle-aged and older people are the principal sufferers of Alzheimer's disease and other forms of dementia. More than

100 000 people suffer from dementia in Australia tody. Most of them are over sixty years old, although the problem can begin when people are still in their forties or fifties, or even younger.

'Senility' was once the common term for serious loss of memory, as if it were a normal part of ageing. But, as the Alzheimer's Association points out, more people in the over sixty-five age group have cancer than dementia, and no-one would say cancer is a normal part of growing old.

> 'Senility' was once the common term for serious loss of memory, as if it were a normal part of ageing.

Alzheimer's (named after the German neurologist who described the brain changes characteristic of this disease) accounts for more than half of all cases of dementia. Up to the age of sixty-five one person in 1000 is affected, between sixty-five and seventy, one in twenty-five. From seventy to eighty the figure rises to one in ten, and over eighty to one in four. It is incurable, but a great deal of research is being done to unravel its secrets.

The onset of Alzheimer's is usually gradual, with symptoms appearing slowly: forgetfulness, confusion and inability to participate. The reality can be very difficult to acknowledge, but once family and friends can accept what is happening, they tend to find they can take more appropriate action.

Early advice should be sought from the local doctor, welfare staff at the local Council and the Alzheimer's Association. Experience of some people is that it may be better to remind disoriented people constantly about the reality around them, than to play along with their mistakes and fantasies. This is best done in a low-key way, by slipping basic information into the conversation. Of course while this approach can work well with some people, it may not be appropriate for everyone.

The four 'Ws' are a helpful reminder:
- Who – use the person's name, and your own name, reminding him or her of your relationship, and who their family members are.

- Where – mention the town, whose house it is, what room.
- What – explain what you're doing, especially when you need some co-operation.
- When – name the day of the week, and season of the year, refer to the person's age.

The Alzheimer's Association suggests many ways of cheering up a person with dementia: singing old songs together, affectionate physical contact, outings to familiar places, visits from old friends and the companionship of pets. There are many other activities that can be productive. Your local Association can give you more ideas.

How well and how long you, as a carer, are able to cope with the effects of dementia depends on a number of things, such as your own age and health, what kinds of help and support are available, whether you are a wage earner, looking after a family or living on the pension.

> Carers, no matter what the condition of the one being cared for, need understanding, sympathy, and respite themselves.

The Home and Community Care Programme operating in each state offers a range of basic support services that enable people to live at home as long as possible. These include home help, personal care with bathing and dressing, home maintenance, food services, transport, community respite care and paramedical services.

Even so, the principal carer is usually a close family member, often a spouse. It can be very useful for the carer to meet others in similar circumstances through a carers support group. These are arranged regularly by Alzheimer's Associations across Australia, and there is a freecall number to enable you to find out where you can attend.*

Carers, no matter what the condition of the one being cared for, form one of the largest armies of volunteers in the country, and need understanding, sympathy, and respite themselves. Carers of dementia sufferers, and the physically disabled in particular, appear to have higher levels of depressive and other common psychological symptoms.

As the one cared for deteriorates still further, the time comes for letting go. This is stressful for all concerned, and again support and guidance will help. If the family have discussed the possibility of such an event well in advance, the wishes and needs of all concerned will be better handled. In the case of many ageing diseases, an Aged Care Assessment Team – one of the many established by the Commonwealth Government in 1985 – will assist the family in deciding on and arranging for the most suitable future care of the patient. That care could be in a hostel, special care unit or a nursing home.

Incontinence has been described by many as life's most embarrassing problem. About 800 000 adult Australians are said to have bladder control problems, which distress and humiliate them, yet fewer than one in ten are actually treated. Women are seven or eight times more likely to have the problem, although elderly men and women seem to be equally affected, and the severity of incontinence increases with age.

> Incontinence has been described by many as life's most embarrassing problem.

A growing number of men in the forty-five to sixty-five age group, many of whom have had a prostatectomy, suffer from incontinence, but respond quite well to pelvic floor exercises. Menopause is another milestone that affects a woman's continence. Almost ten per cent of women date the onset of their leakage problem from the time of hysterectomy. Up to forty per cent of people over seventy-five develop bladder control problems. This has less to do with age per se and more to do with factors such as decreased mobility, increased medication consumption and the concurrence of other medical problems that may occur with ageing.

The Continence Foundation of Australia* assures us that most incontinence can be cured or at least significantly improved. The condition is not normal at any age after infancy. There is, however, no miracle cure guaranteed to put everyone right. The

Foundation produces a regular newsletter VOICE (Victory over incontinence/continence education) financially supported by the Department of Veterans Affairs.

According to the Foundation's patron, the writer and neurophysiologist Dr Colleen McCullough, the main reason people hide incontinence is that they think of themselves as a laughing stock. 'The time to start dealing with incontinence is early on, before it becomes a serious embarrassment affecting everybody around the sufferer', she writes. 'There *are* things we can do about bladder control problems, so why wait until it becomes a major difficulty? The Continence Foundation is the place to turn, so turn to it!'

There are four simple steps everyone should take to keep the bladder healthy:

1 Maintain a good fluid intake, of at least 1.5 litres of water (six to eight cups) per day. Limit the amount of caffeine as this irritates the bladder. Instant coffee contains less caffeine than percolated; tea contains less caffeine than coffee, and is actually much stronger as a diuretic. Limit the amount of alcohol as it may make the brain less able to co-ordinate bladder control. It also causes an irritable bladder.

2 Practise good toilet habits. Take time emptying your bladder so it empties completely. Avoid the habit of going 'just in case', as this tends to result in the bladder developing a smaller capacity. Wait until you NEED to go. Going to the toilet before going out or going to bed is of course fine. It is normal to go to the toilet about six to eight times a day, and for older people twice in the night.

3 Maintain good bowel habits. Keep regular and avoid constipation. Persistent straining can weaken the pelvic floor muscles. Many people find that constipation exacerbates their incontinence. Bowel (faecal) incontinence must never be accepted as normal. It is preventable and curable.

4 Look after your pelvic floor muscles. Keep the tone strong by regular pelvic floor exercise. Being overweight is an extra weight for this area to carry.

Seek help from a health professional if you have difficulty with any of these steps.

Treatment can be either conservative (meaning 'interfering as little as possible') or surgical. The main types of incontinence, and their treatment are the following:

- **Stress incontinence:** involuntary loss (that is urine leaking out of the bladder without the owner's permission) immediately associated with coughing, sneezing, lifting, straining, bending or other physical exertion. Weakness of the sphincter muscles and the muscles of the pelvic floor may be damaged by childbirth, straining to evacuate the constipated bowel, and the menopause. There are a number of medications that have an adverse effect on the bladder and bowel function, for example some medications for the control of high blood pressure.
  Treatment: in the first instance, weight loss and pelvic floor exercises. By following a course of these properly and conscientiously performed exercises – if necessary with the help of a physiotherapist – seventy per cent of women with stress incontinence can cure or significantly improve their condition.
- **Urge incontinence:** involuntary loss of urine associated with a strong desire to urinate, and the sufferer is unable to get to the toilet in time.
  Treatment: as there are many factors that can cause urge incontinence, treatment consists of addressing the underlying cause. Medication can calm the bladder muscle, especially if allied with bladder re-training techniques. Drug therapy can be quite effective in elderly people.
- **Dribble incontinence:** leaking of urine without warning or provocation.
  Treatment: again, treatment depends on the cause. If the dribbling is caused by weak sphincter muscles (as may occur after a prostatectomy), the dribble problem may be resolved with pelvic floor exercises. Again, it is important to see a specialist who can help determine the most appropriate intervention.

- **Overflow incontinence:** involuntary loss of urine associated with a chronically distended and overfull bladder.
  Treatment: the underlying cause must be addressed. Medication may be prescribed. In some cases the person may be taught special techniques to properly empty the bladder.

When incontinence is difficult to cure, protective pads, pants and appliances for both male and female sufferers are invaluable. Informative pamphlets are available from pharmacies, doctors' surgeries and district nursing services. Some funding schemes are available to assist with the purchase of some products. Contact your local continence service for further information. Overall, the promotion of continence among older people is helped by an active interest in daily life, keeping weight within normal limits, and ensuring a daily fluid intake of six to eight cups of water, with decreasing amounts of caffeine. Nurse consultants are available at the Continence Resource Centre in your state, to discuss any questions or concerns you may have, in a friendly and sensitive way.

The Continence Foundation of Australia in 1995 negotiated a merger with US TOO International Inc. to provide a support network of groups linking prostate cancer and prostate disease survivors with the health care community. Since prostate problems may cause severe incontinence problems, the aims and objectives of the two organisations are complementary. US TOO Australia has as its motto 'Learning to Cope through Knowledge and Hope', and it therefore stresses the importance of self-help groups in the healing process.

In short ...

1 Consider your definition of 'wellness' – use this as your own individual benchmark for how you aim to feel every day.

2 When you think of diet, think of moderation ... and don't forget the fibre!

3 You don't have to be affluent to live well.

4 Being overweight is a health hazard.

5 Prevention is more than half the battle.

6 You don't have to sweat and strain when you exercise – you should be able to whistle while you're doing it, and chatting to a friend is even better.

7 If you look good, the chances are you'll feel good.

8 Don't be afraid to make reasonable human claims for yourself if you are caring for a needy person.

9 Be courageous enough to make changes to your lifestyle to help you relieve stress and anxiety. Remember that relaxing requires effort – this is not as silly as it sounds.

10 Drug use and abuse doesn't apply only to illegal substances.

11 Don't anticipate the worst.

12 Enjoy your accumulated wisdom, and the spin-offs.

7
Health and gender difference

Men die younger than women. Their life span is now about seven years less than the eighty years most Australian women may expect to reach. The projection is that women over the age of eighty will outnumber men by more than two to one soon after the turn of the century. There will be 300 000 women aged over eighty-five in the year 2031. They nevertheless get 'sicker' often, they occupy more hospital beds, take more tranquillisers and sedatives and have a higher rate of some mental and physical disorders. Women die, as men do, of heart disease, cancer, strokes and accidents, and yet they live longer than men. The question has to be asked, Why? Is it simply because they look after themselves better, go to the doctor and the chemist, and use the health care system more often?

Is men's propensity for risk taking, and therefore for accidents, an issue? Is men's overt risk behaviour of smoking and drinking another factor? Do we agree with psychologist/writer Bettina Arndt that masculinity itself is a health hazard? Is women's capacity to confide in others about their health problems a help?

Are genetic or other factors the key? Researchers as yet have no clear answers, but some significant studies are under way in Australia.

Colin Mathers of the Australian Institute of Health in Canberra offered five types of reasons at the Men's Health Summit in Melbourne in 1995, to account for sex differences in health. There were biological risks and acquired risks. Others were illness behaviour, health reporting behaviour and prior health care.

Men's health

Oh! that we had more of the gerontocrats, those healthy seventy-year-old men identified twenty-five years ago by two specialists at the Prince of Wales Hospital in Sydney, Dr P. Beaumont and Professor Fred Hollows. The gerontocrat was the retired man at seventy or over who was free from vascular disease and sometimes younger in mind and body than a fifty-year-old. 'We are as old as our vessels are', it used to be said. Amazingly well and well-adjusted people, the gerontocrats had not allowed themselves to be browbeaten into thinking they were old.

> 'We are as old as our vessels are', it used to be said. Amazingly well and well-adjusted people, the gerontocrats had not allowed themselves to be browbeaten into thinking they were old.

The gerontocrats undertook medical, physiological, biochemical and psychological tests, were questioned about how they lived, what they ate, their smoking, drinking, and sexual habits and their general attitude towards life. They all had the ability to dissolve clots in blood vessels. None led a passive, monotonous or uninvolved existence. All were contented and happy, busy or even busier than when they were in paid employment. Dr Beaumont foretold that the careful, moderate, positive thinking thirty- or forty-year old person might become the gerontocrat of tomorrow. How many people over sixty-five whom you know would you describe as gerontocrats?

Men's health became the subject of the National Summit in Melbourne in August 1995, the first of its kind to be held in Australia. It was sponsored by the Commonwealth Department of Human Services and Health as a first step to generating discussion and debate about men's health.

As a result of the conference, the Primary Health Care Group within the Commonwealth Department of Human Services and Health is now developing a national men's health policy. Another significant outcome is the establishment of the first post-graduate course in men's health, initiated by psychologist Mr Allan Huggins and due to commence at Curtin University in Western Australia in 1996.

The *Age* health writer, Steve Dow, reported when the summit began, that 'man is under siege'. He is destined to live a shorter life than woman, more likely to get drunk, run his car off the road, have a heart attack, die from smoking, or commit suicide. 'And don't even mention prostate cancer', wrote Dow. 'He won't.'

This is part of the problem. Men visit the doctor less, and this appears to be related to social conditioning. A useful question to ask is: 'Did your *father* take *you* to visit the doctor?'

Older men's health was given prominence by Dr John McCallum, head of Health Science at the University of Western Sydney. Dr McCallum discussed the contradictory differences on successful ageing of older men, stressing that while all the major causes of death were higher for men than for women, men used the services of primary health care less than women.

Dr McCallum stated that this difference in using health services related to the male sex role, and communication failures between doctor and patient. The male predilection for stoicism, the suppression of the feminine, restricted emotional expression, self-reliance, the pursuit of money and status, and homophobia, all play a part in this.

Associate Professor Edmond Chiu conducts the Academic Unit in the Psychiatry of Old Age at the University of Melbourne, and the title of talks he often gives is 'Old Men Don't Cry'. 'Men are taught to be brave and strong; that is what their mothers taught them', Dr Chiu explains.

> Coming from a Chinese background, where matriarchy is venerated, I know all about this. Grandmothers' wisdom is particularly respected – the hand that rocks the cradle truly does rule the Chinese. I continually see Australian men who have been socialised to be stoical; the stiff upper lip is much in evidence, and the bush tradition of never complaining is still alive and well. 'Whingeing' is considered a bad thing for men.

Dr Chiu believes therefore that men are disadvantaged in terms of their health because they have not been allowed to admit to being sick. They suffer in silence, then when they do visit a GP or a psychiatrist it is often very late in their illness.

He argued that little is spent on specific men's health programmes in this country. Much may be spent on *diseases* of men, he stated, but 'men's health programmes', specific to them as *persons*, are few compared to the number of women's health programmes.

Mr Richard Fletcher, a leading health educator from the University of Newcastle, speaking at the National Summit, was able to claim nevertheless that Australia is a world leader in awareness and community approaches to men's health issues. It was in fact grass-roots awareness that led to the creation of the National Men's Health Conference. Mr Fletcher served on its Advisory Committee. He told the conference that Australia was more developed and on a better footing than the United Kingdom. He had attended Britain's first National Men's Health Conference, and was therefore able to make first-hand comparisons.

> 'Men are taught to be brave and strong. I continually see Australian men who have been socialised to be stoical; "Whingeing" is considered a bad thing for men.'

While men are living longer, women are increasing their longevity more, with the four-year gap in average age of death earlier this century now more than six years. Men sixty-five and over die at a rate sixty-one per cent higher than older women, with lung cancer almost four times as high and suicide almost three times as high. Men in fact suffer in excess of women in all the leading cancers that are not female specific – lung, colon, bladder, rectum and stomach. As Steve Dow reported, men everywhere are now poised to have a say. 'Whether the social conditioning of the Australian male will allow them to do so is another question.'

Dr Garry Egger, a behavioural scientist at the University of Newcastle, has devised the successful Gutbuster programme aimed at middle-aged men with pot bellies. He began with the fact that forty-two per cent of Australian men have abdominal obesity, and are therefore at risk for cardiovascular disease, late-onset diabetes and other diseases. The problem is increasing as our society becomes more affluent. He estimates that sixty-five to seventy per cent of Australian men over fifty are overweight or obese, and the majority of these are abdominally obese. His waist-loss programme, in which overweight men take part in a six-week project to change their lifestyle, has helped 16 000 men in three years to reduce their waist size by one per cent per week.

> Dr Garry Egger began with the fact that forty-two per cent of Australian men have abdominal obesity.

Courses, supported by the Gutbusters Scientific Advisory Board, a group of experts in health, medicine and nutrition, are now conducted in every capital city, and a number of regional centres. For those unable to attend in person, there is a correspondence course available through the Gutbusters head office.* Dr Egger stresses that men have physiological as well as psychological advantages in fat loss. 'The way to a man's head (if not his heart or liver or other suffering organs) may well be through his stomach', he told the Men's Health Summit.

> 'The way to a man's head (if not his heart or liver or other suffering organs) may well be through his stomach.'

Gutbusters is the first public health programme to attract Australian men. Even so, Dr Egger states it is not easy to 'get them in'. Fifty per cent of those who do attend are persuaded by their wives to do so, the rest are persuaded either by their peers, or by 'the advertisement they've been carrying around for twelve months'. The programme is now being taken overseas, with Dr Egger making it available through the European Conference on Obesity. Advice to all men, especially those over fifty, is to educate themselves on the facts of fat loss, to have a high-fibre, low-fat diet, and to 'get moving'.

The Testicular Cancer Prevention Project, initiated by Apex Clubs around Australia, was commended, as was the establishment by health workers in western Sydney of a Men's Health Forum. Just as women are advised to practise breast self-examination regularly, so, too, are men over forty encouraged to practise testicular self-examination once a month.

A national toll-free telephone service has been established to answer questions about men's health issues, particularly prostate disease. The service, known as Prostate Info-Line,* is operated by the Pharmaceutical Society of Australia, which distributes a 'prostate problems' fact card through Self Care pharmacies.

Some cleverly planned programmes to entice men to consider health issues were devised in rural Victoria in 1993. Titled 'A Men's Night Out', they were organised by a community health nurse in Charlton, Anne Donaldson, to provide information to men on matters like stress, heart disease and prostate problems. The idea of the relaxed, informative, social evening – for men only – proved so successful that other country towns quickly copied the idea as being too good to miss, and thus proved that 'real men' were prepared to accept the advice of credible speakers. Many community health centres now provide similar programmes, utilising similar 'grape vine' strategies to get the message out. One important lesson learned was to have experts who speak the language of rural people – simple, straightforward and with a dose of humour!

A draft national men's health policy, based on contributions at the first Men's Health Summit in 1995, was launched by the Federal Government early in 1996. It plans to target the needs of rural men, along with other specific population groups such as gay men and men from non-English speaking backgrounds. Many rural men, socialised to be strong and in control, suffer in silence rather than seeking assistance. At the same time many have difficulties in getting away from their multitudinous tasks on the farm, and health and welfare services are just too far away.

Instead of focusing just on illnesses, strategies were announced to consider how a man's life influences the issues that have an impact on his health. There will be a strong emphasis on encouraging men to become actively involved in the management of health and safety in their workplace. By doing this, men may be motivated to manage their own general health more actively.

> There will be a strong emphasis on encouraging men to become actively involved in the management of health and safety in their workplace.

The draft policy acknowledges that retirement is a key health influence for older men. The national action plan seeks to promote and develop a role for existing service organisations like the RSL and Rotary, to help promote initiatives that will make a qualitative difference to older men's lives.

The draft men's health policy also notes the role older men have in caring, both for themselves and for others. Many men who are widowed or who take on the role of carer have little knowledge of good nutrition, because they have previously relied on their spouse for this. One in three carers is a male, the report states, and forty-two per cent of these are over sixty-five years. Balancing what is often a new role with consideration of their own health creates particular issues for these men.

> One in three carers is a male, the report states, and forty-two per cent of these are over sixty-five years.

Women's health

The most recent publication by the Australian Bureau of Statistics on women's health (December 1994) shows that females consumed in the vicinity of sixty per cent of health expenditure (that is capital and recurrent) in 1992–93. The latest sex split figures (1989–90) showed women outnumbered men in the use of the four main items of total recurrent expenditure, in hospitals, nursing homes, medical services and pharmaceuticals.

Some women's groups, however, have argued that more money has been spent on specific male conditions. Between 1985 and 1989 for example, the Medical Research Committee of the National Health and Medical Research Council of Australia allocated 2.4 per cent of its expenditure to women's health projects. Most of these were devoted to pregnancy, family planning and menopause.

The Key Centre for Women's Health in Society* was established in 1988 within the Faculty of Medicine at the University of Melbourne. The Centre grew out of the feminist-led women's health movement, where it was recognised that the social conditions that surround women and impinge on their health differed from those of men. The Centre is unique in integrating knowledge from the social sciences and humanities with that of medicine. Its main areas of activity are in research, teaching, community consultation and in running educational programmes. It takes its motto from the words of the nineteenth-century philosopher John Stuart Mill: 'No understanding of women will ever be possible until women themselves begin to tell what they know'.

> John Stuart Mill: 'No understanding of women will ever be possible until women themselves begin to tell what they know.'

There are four objectives underpinning all of the Centre's activities. They are to:
- *encourage* positive changes in the delivery of women's health services

- *empower* women to care for their own health
- *increase* expertise in the area of women's health research
- *develop* and promote a research model defined by women and embracing a number of disciplines.

A significant development at the Key Centre is the Alma Unit on Women and Ageing, founded in 1993 to consider the particular problems and issues that older women face. The project has been made possible by the generosity of Ms Fleur Spitzer, who is providing core money for three years to employ a teaching and research unit. The unit is named after Fleur's mother, Alma, a model of vitality and involvement for all of her ninety-four years. Betty Friedan launched the Alma Unit during her visit to Melbourne in March 1994.

The Alma Unit is Australia's first multi-disciplinary teaching and research unit focusing on the lives of women. Fleur Spitzer is associated with the organisation Women in Philanthropy, and she wants to encourage what she calls 'focused giving', through endowments and donations to a cause they believe in. Her own focus is that stage of life after sixty, which can be rich and full, a stage where family and work commitments are no longer as important, and other interests can flourish.

'With the changing composition of the population, it is important to investigate older women's experiences and encourage a view that doesn't see old age as a disease', she states. 'We should view it as simply another stage in life, a stage in which women have a lot to offer our society.' She is enjoying her own 'third stage' to the full.

Susan Feldman, project director of the Alma Unit, stresses the need to be realistic about the limitations that age can put upon us, without seeing them as an impediment. The Alma project focuses on issues surrounding older women's quality of life, and what their experience of ageing actually is. Many women have been marginalised all their lives and the 'golden age' remains a myth. Ageing homeless, disabled and Aboriginal women all have specific issues until now largely unaddressed.

The Alma Unit has been reviewing research already done in the area of older women's health. Susan has found that much of this research focuses on ill-health, disease or incapacity, often disregarding the complexity and richness of women's lives. She herself is continually amazed at the enormous variation in older women's experiences. What strikes her forcibly is the increased diversity of women's lives.

'Existing research often portrays ageing people as an homogenous group', she writes, 'ignoring the differences between the experiences of a sixty-five-year-old woman and an eighty-five-year-old woman. They are not only from two different generations but also have different experiences of, and perspectives on, ageing.'

She is seeing a correlation between who we are when younger, regarding our attitudes to life and our health, and who we are when older. Older women's wellbeing is the result of choices and decisions made throughout their lives, and women of every age are needing to recognise the long-term implications of these choices and events. This is not to underestimate the significance of events over which women have only limited control.

A significant study currently under way at the Key Centre is the Women's Midlife Health Project, which obviously includes a study of menopause. It is the first study of its kind in Australia, and one of very few worldwide. It is considering not only the physiological changes, such as hormone levels, of the menopause, but other biological, psychological and social factors on women's health and wellbeing, including the changes in work, family life and sexual functioning that are so often overlooked.

Two thousand of the 2750 women aged 45–55 who were initially approached were interviewed. Those who had not already experienced menopause, had not had surgery to remove their uterus and were not using oral contraceptives, were asked if they would participate further, and 494 agreed to participate in the first round. In the second round, 474 are continuing. Most are interviewed in their own homes.

The Centre hopes to stay in touch with these women as they proceed through their midlife years, especially looking at how and why health and wellbeing changes, and what has triggered those changes. Blood samples are basic to the study, and the Australian Dairy Corporation is funding another important aspect, in enabling all women in the study to have their bone density measured.

The third stage of the project is looking specifically at physical activity and diet, to determine how these may relate to midlife health. The team hopes eventually to produce exercise and dietary guidelines especially for women.

Overall, the preliminary results of the entire project are looking very positive. For the most part, the women seemed to be in good health. Contrary to some common beliefs, most women have said they did not worry about being too old to have children, nor were they worried about being less attractive. Although about half the women interviewed thought that some women in midlife get depressed or irritable, most believed that women with many interests in their lives hardly noticed menopause.

> Adjusting to an 'empty nest' in midlife, so often thought to be difficult for women when their children leave home, was shown by two-thirds of the women to be of no concern.

Adjusting to an 'empty nest' in midlife, so often thought to be difficult for women when their children leave home, was shown by two-thirds of the women to be of no concern. Fewer than half said some women believed they were no longer 'real' women after menopause. Two-thirds thought few women regretted the cessation of their periods. A similar proportion said that most or some women believed that menopause causes no important changes.

Menopause Clinics and Midlife Clinics now operate in many of the major metropolitan hospitals, and they, with the family doctor, can offer good advice. Many centres arrange discussion groups for women to share their experiences about this stage of life.

Menopause may be called the universal women's experience, but it is not experienced by women in a universal way. Their experience varies greatly across the world. Dr Julia Shelley, who is associated with the Melbourne Women's Midlife Health Project at the University of Melbourne, believes menopause is as much a social experience as a physical one. She maintains that as a society Australians are disparaging of menopause. It is seen as a marker of ageing in women.

In Australia, the menopause experience varies. During the menopause the ovaries lower the production of oestrogen and progesterone, and menstruation ceases. It usually happens between the ages of forty-five and fifty-five; the average age is fifty-one. Some women (an estimated twenty per cent) have no problems, some have severe (an estimated ten per cent) problems, and the rest have a few problems.

Symptoms can occur up to five years before menstruation ends. The Women's Midlife Health studies and other studies have found that hot flushes, night sweats and vaginal symptoms are the only ones strictly menopausal. Women, however, do report other symptoms such as sleep disturbance, poor bladder control, feeling 'down', snappy or irritable and crying spells.

The low oestrogen levels, which play such a key part in the onset of osteoporosis, also lead to changes in the skin. The elasticity goes, and the skin feels, and becomes, thinner. Women are to some extent protected against heart disease, and possibly strokes, by the oestrogen their ovaries produce. Diet, particularly a low-fat diet rich in fibre and calcium, is important not only to control weight at this time; it also keeps cholesterol levels within desirable limits. Exercise is also imperative.

One of the great medical/scientific controversies for menopausal women concerns hormone replacement therapy (HRT).

There is no definitive answer about the benefits and risks of HRT, hence whether women should take it or not. For a balanced view, researchers involved in the Melbourne Women's Midlife Health Project at the University of Melbourne are a reliable source of information.

> There is no definitive answer about the benefits and risks of HRT, hence whether women should take it or not.

Dr Julia Shelley is an epidemiologist whose research interests include hormone therapy and Pap smear screening. She has written the following in one of the Key Centre's recent newsletters:

> There are really two issues we should consider when looking at HRT. The first are the scientific implications. What are the medical benefits and what are the health risks involved in taking HRT?
>
> Secondly, and perhaps more importantly, are the social issues. Is HRT being sold as a cure for old age? Are we responding to fears about loss of sexual attractiveness after the menopause? Are we prepared to take hormonal medication daily for long periods of time? There are a lot of question marks surrounding the use of HRT. We do not even know how many women are using it although we know it is on the increase.
>
> There are obvious and clear benefits of HRT. We know it can control such symptoms as hot flushes and some studies have shown that it can help the long-term problems of osteoporosis and heart disease. On the negative side oestrogen therapy [alone] has been linked with uterine cancer and there is some evidence of increased risk of breast cancer. Erratic periods, weight gain and breast tenderness are other possible side-effects.
>
> It is currently very hard for women to make informed judgements about HRT because of the lack of information. Part of the push for the use of HRT is coming from companies who stand to gain a lot from extensive and long-term use by women. We need to evaluate what the effect of HRT use will be on women's lives, what the benefits and the risks are and to explore the social questions.

Dr Shelley adds that while HRT is not a new drug (having been used since the 1940s), its preventative focus is new. Women considering taking HRT as a preventative measure against possible future health problems, such as heart disease and osteoporosis, are demanding more information about its possible risks and benefits. This information is crucial to the decision.

Dr Shelley refers further to women's need for reliable information:

> Many doctors believe that more women will take HRT if they are better educated about its benefits. At the same time there is a growing school of thought against the widespread use of it, particularly for preventative purposes. Conflicting messages are creating uncertainty and even guilt in some women who feel they should be taking it, but do not like the side-effects or the fact that they have to take pills every day.

These side-effects include fluid retention, nausea, weight gain and sore breasts. In women without hysterectomies, unusual bleeding patterns are a problem and must be examined in case they are caused by other complications.

Dr Elizabeth Farrell, who has co-authored the successful *The HRT Handbook*,* is optimistic about HRT. A gynaecologist who set up the first menopause clinic at Melbourne's Queen Victoria Hospital in 1982, she describes the menopause transition as an important phase, for it is a time of relief, release and pain.

The menopause releases women from the cloak of reproduction; many women see it as a relief from the monthly period, and for many there is pain in realising it is the beginning of the ageing process. Dr Farrell quotes the French proverb 'Forty is the old age of youth, fifty is the youth of old age'.

> Women may be feeling the loss of youth at this time, but it is also the time to adjust, to come to grips with this new phase, to reappraise the time and opportunities that lie before them.
>
> A lot of women forget their own needs ... I think they should feel they have the right after menopausal transition to reward themselves, to focus on themselves. This means they should feel

free to choose options, and one of these options is the use of HRT. They must seek both information and education, however, for HRT treatment is long-term, lasting from five to perhaps twenty years.

Nearly all women are able to take HRT, although certain conditions require specialist treatment before therapy can be considered safe. These conditions include cancer of the breast or uterus, a recent history of blood clots, severe liver disease or undiagnosed vaginal bleeding. HRT is most commonly taken by (daily) tablets of natural oestrogen.

The menopausal women whom doctors see are mostly those who suffer with severe hot flushes, mood swings, irritability, and night stress. An enormous number of women seek natural therapies, says Dr Farrell. 'These women need to understand that natural therapies, too, are medicines and are *not* harmless. The treatment is not something you can pick up off the shelf at a health food shop. Many women prefer natural therapies, but they must be used under the guidance of an appropriately trained naturopath or alternative therapist.'

Dr Farrell adds that dietary oestrogens are becoming extremely important for women in menopausal transition. They have implications for improving protection against heart disease and osteoporosis. They are to be found in the diets followed by vegetarians: soy products, cereals, bran, wheat germ, alfalfa, beans, legumes, stone fruit, hops, barley and sesame seeds, and in the oestrogen-containing herbs like sage, chervil, dill, caraway, basil, garlic and parsley.

Testosterone replacement therapy is appropriate when there is a loss of libido, or sex drive, Dr Farrell adds. Adequate oestrogen therapy may also improve the sexual response and eliminate any discomfort of intercourse. In some women three monthly injections of testosterone or a testosterone implant once or twice a year helps their sex drive, without any 'male' side-effects.

For women who suffer in the menopausal transition and after, particularly when they have physical symptoms (such as hot flushes) interfering with their quality of life, they should know about all their options for treatment. These options include good diet, exercise, natural therapies or hormone replacement. Women should feel free to make a choice or to perhaps use one or all of the options available to them for good health.

> ## In short ...
>
> **1** The question of why the female lifespan is longer than that of the male needs to be addressed. And who better to do it than men?
>
> **2** Social conditioning could very well be a factor in men visiting the doctor less than women. Maybe this could be overcome by fathers sharing the role of taking children to the doctor, especially their sons.
>
> **3** Stoicism is another possible result of social conditioning: Real men can't admit to being sick?
>
> **4** Abdominal obesity – the pot belly – affects forty-two per cent of Australian men, a costly, unsightly and hazardous condition. Try Gutbusters!
>
> **5** Retirement is a key issue for older men, so prepare creatively for it.
>
> **6** Women are becoming increasingly responsible for the quality of their own health programmes.
>
> **7** Older women, and men, need to be encouraged to see old age as simply another stage of life, not a disease. Of course, it would be useful if younger people shared this view, since they will reach it too.
>
> **8** Menopause is an individual as well as a universal women's experience, and is still surrounded by many myths.

8
Beating the statistics

Lay people tend to talk and think of cancer as one disease when in fact there are more than one hundred variations. Because it is predominantly a disease of older groups, and may be the result of risk-taking in earlier years, we must consider cancer in some detail here.

In 1907 cancer was the eighth most common cause of death; in 1947 it was second only to cardiovascular disease, and it remains so today. Because many cancers are attributable to lifestyle or environmental factors, it has been realistically estimated that one-third of the cancers in Australia could be prevented by feasible programmes, and more are potentially preventable. Prevention, however complex, is therefore the great imperative.

Four overall strategies for *primary prevention of cancer* are now in place in Australia. They are:

- reducing tobacco consumption
- adopting a prudent diet
- reducing alcohol intake
- reducing sun exposure

The importance of meditation, and time given to reflection, are other preventative methods. A balanced life, which promotes the functioning of the immune system at its peak, is always to be sought.

There are Anti-Cancer Councils, Funds, or Foundations in every Australian state and territory, with volunteer units and support groups in great numbers, in city and country alike, and the Australian Cancer Society has a toll-free number for its Cancer Information Service,* nation-wide.

Diet and cancer

The first statement to make is that diet is considered to be a major cause of human cancer. This is supported by the Anti-Cancer Council. While estimates range between ten and seventy per cent, there is widespread acceptance that about thirty-five per cent of cancers in modern industrialised societies are caused by dietary factors.

The investigation of diet and cancer has nevertheless been plagued by problems that only the medical and academic communities can explain. Other aspects of one's life, such as physical activity and personal attributes, interact with dietary factors. One can merely generalise here, and again use the National Cancer Prevention Policy guidelines. Those cancer sites considered to be related to diet are the stomach and large bowel, breast, prostate and endometrium, the lung and cervix. All make up the majority of cancers occurring among Australians.

> Diet is considered to be a major cause of human cancer.

The strongest and most consistent evidence for cancer protection relates to the overall consumption of fruit and vegetables, although certain vegetable groups seem to have an important effect in their own right. For example, the brassica group, cabbage, broccoli, cauliflower, brussels sprouts, mustard greens, turnips and kohlrabi are thought to protect against cancer of the large bowel. Leafy green and yellow and orange vegetables, including spinach, silverbeet, carrots, pumpkin and sweet potato are associated with reduced risks of cancers of the lung, oesophagus, cervix and larynx. Fruit, especially citrus fruit, contains vitamin C, which is believed to reduce the risk of cancers of the stomach and oesophagus.

Cereals, including wheat, barley, rice, rye, corn and oats, all of which contain complex carbohydrates and fibre, have been associated — if somewhat inconsistently — with a reduced risk of bowel and breast cancer. Being overweight, the precursor to obesity, should always be avoided. The recommended Australian guideline, *to maintain a healthy body weight by balancing physical activity with food intake*, is pertinent to cancer prevention.

Given the established risk of head, neck and liver cancer associated with alcohol consumption, limited intake is highly recommended. Women should limit their drinking habits, given the increasingly consistent evidence that moderate to high levels of alcohol may increase the risk of breast cancer.

Colorectal cancer

Colorectal cancer (CRC), that is cancer of the large bowel, is the most common internal malignancy in Australia. One Australian in twenty-five is destined to develop CRC at some stage of life on current estimates. From 1973 to 1991 the incidence of CRC increased steadily among males, and although the incidence in females increased up to 1985, it decreased thereafter. In 1991 in New South Wales, CRC was the second-most common cause of death from cancer, after lung cancer.

The bad news is that beyond the age of fifty the incidence of CRC increases rapidly, and for men aged eighty-five or older it rises to 5 per 1000, for women 4 per 1000. The good news is that the prognosis for CRC patients is relatively good, compared with that for lung and stomach cancer. Surgical treatment of early detected CRC is highly successful; the difficulty is finding it early enough. Any bowel bleeding or other irregular bowel activity should be diagnosed immediately. Most at risk are those with a family history of CRC.

Because suspicion falls also on diet as a factor, as shown above, the dietary guidelines of the National Better Health Programme should be followed.

Skin cancers

Australia has a doubtful claim to fame: the highest rate of skin cancer in the world. It is our most common type of cancer. Although the fatality rate is relatively low — at about 1000 per year — skin cancers are important because of their large demands on preventive and curative services. Early detection and appropriate management are as usual of prime importance, for 99 per cent of skin cancers can be cured. Left untreated, they can be lethal.

Reducing the nature and amount of exposure to sunlight is one of the principal goals of the National Cancer Prevention Policy. It is expected that by the year 2000 the vast majority of Australians should understand the nature of skin cancer and its causes; the prevalence of sunburn during summer should be substantially reduced, with sun exposure reduced by at least twenty per cent of the 1990 levels.

> Skin cancer is our most common type of cancer.

Sun avoidance between the hours 10 a.m. and 2 p.m. (or 11 a.m. to 3 p.m. daylight saving time) will remain the key strategy for individuals. They will be encouraged to seek shade wherever possible, and to create shade around the home by constructing canopies or planting shade trees. They will also need to wear protective clothing including broad-brimmed hats, shirts with long sleeves and long trousers, all with fabrics sufficiently densely woven to cast a deep shadow when held up to the light.

The use of sunscreens is an integral part of the precautions recommended to prevent skin cancer in Australia. A broad spectrum sunscreen marked 'Maximum Protection 15+' offers the best protection. It is, however, an adjunct to natural protection, not a substitute for it. Sunglasses should be the close-fitting, wrap-around type, and labelled according to the Standards Association of Australia standard (AS – 1067).

People should be alert for any new spot, freckle, or mole that is changing in thickness, colour or shape over a period of weeks or months, changes to an existing one, or a sore that does not heal, and see their doctor straight away.

The National Cancer Prevention Policy seeks to alter the fashion for suntan, suggests minimum exposure to sunlight for workers by rescheduling work outside the danger hours, recommends outdoor and sporting activities early or late in the day, and education programmes to discourage the use of solariums. Community planting of trees in schools and other public places should incorporate shade creation.

> The National Cancer Prevention Policy seeks to alter the fashion for suntan.

Information leaflets are available from clinics and doctors' waiting rooms.

Cancer of the breast

After skin cancer, cancer of the breast is the most common cancer among Australian women. The mortality rate in Australia in 1993 was 2641, that is five per cent of all female deaths, and eighteen per cent of female cancer deaths. In 1988, the most recent year for which national figures are available, 6542 cases of breast cancer were reported in Australian women. This makes breast cancer twice as common as cancer of the colon. One in fifteen Australian women will develop breast cancer at some time in their lives. The incidence rises rapidly from the early twenties to fifty years of age, and after a brief plateau rises steadily thereafter.

Breast cancer is also the most common cause of death from cancer in Australian women. In 1988, 2348 deaths were recorded, that is over eighteen per cent of all female cancer deaths recorded that year. From this mortality data, the likelihood of a woman dying from breast cancer before the age of seventy-five is one in forty-four.

Circumstantial evidence suggests that a diet of less than thirty per cent of kilojoules (kJ) from animal fat may be protective. (There are 4.2 kJ to one calorie.) This is in line with the Australian dietary guidelines which recommend no more than one-third of saturated ('the bad' animal) fat to two-thirds of mono- or poly-saturated ('the good' vegetable) fats. Our total daily energy intake should include thirty to thirty-five per cent fats, fifty to fifty-five per cent carbohydrates and ten to fifteen per cent protein. Current evidence indicates that daily consumption of several glasses of alcoholic beverage moderately increases the risk of female breast cancer.

Monthly breast self-examination (BSE) is a useful method of secondary prevention. It has been found that the tumours detected by women practising BSE tend to be smaller than those in women not practising BSE. A study of almost 90 000 women, initiated by the World Health Organization, showed the average tumour size was 1.3 cm less among the BSE group.

Most breast changes are not a sign of cancer. Most are harmless, for only one lump out of ten will be cancer, but any change should be checked by one's doctor.

The National Cancer Prevention Policy has a goal to ensure the orderly, carefully monitored expansion of mammographic screening, focusing on women aged fifty to sixty-nine years. By the year 2000 it is hoped that all women of this age group will have access to a screening every two years. All women over fifty are encouraged to contact the Australia-wide network of accredited assessment centres for a free mammogram.*

The Queensland Cancer Fund is funding research on hereditary (genetic) factors, which are thought to play a vital role in about five to ten per cent of all breast cancer cases. In these families it appears that an altered gene passed on from parent to child is responsible for a very high chance of developing breast cancer. Although it is not yet possible to isolate this gene, some information about the likelihood of its presence or absence can be gained by doing blood tests on several family members.

The Queensland Institute of Medical Research and the Queen Alexandra Hospital are studying families with a history of breast cancer, and women found to be at high risk are extensively counselled, shown how to do BSE, and examined twice yearly by doctors.

The attitudes of family/spouse/partner are of critical importance in helping women with breast cancer to cope with their physical and psychological problems. Participation in decision-making by both patient and those nearest to her can add greatly to her quality of life. Heart-warming stories are told by survivors in the many Breast Cancer Support Services (BCSS) established around Australia. Ideally, women should help women; husbands and partners help women; parents, siblings and children help women; and all should be able to speak openly about how they feel, whether the feeling is good or bad. The Support Services often use a trained social worker as adviser, and survivors themselves are often the volunteer speakers (in various languages) at all kinds of community forums. Information about your nearest BCSS is available through your state Anti-Cancer Council/Society.

> Ideally, women should help women; husbands and partners help women; parents, siblings and children help women; and all should be able to speak openly about how they feel.

Dr Valerie Clarke, a senior lecturer in psychology at Deakin University who is involved in behavioural research with the Anti-Cancer Council of Victoria, writes:

> I believe that psychological factors play a major part in the early detection of many illnesses and in the course of their treatment. It is essentially a person's beliefs which influence the extent to which they actively promote their own health, and take precautions to ensure the early identification of ill-health. Similarly, our attitudes to an illness influence our response to treatment and our coping with the illness.

> Our attitudes to an illness influence our response to treatment and our coping with the illness.

In a study of thirty breast cancer survivors, with an average age of fifty-four, Dr Clarke and two of her doctoral students found responses from husbands varying between being the major source of support, to being an additional drain on the patient, as difficult as younger children. The report saw the majority of husbands' responses as 'consistent with the traditional stereotypes of the Australian male: of being relatively non-emotional'. It might be, however, the report added, that husbands are reluctant to show their emotions, rather than that they do not experience any.

Older breast cancer survivors, in some cases widowed, found their mature offspring a tower of strength, especially their daughters, and were less concerned about their body image. Those who were widowed had few concerns about the impact of breast cancer on their sexual relations. Older women were more likely to see breast cancer as another practical problem to be dealt with on their journey through life.

Cancer of the cervix

Cancer of the cervix (that is the lower end, or 'neck' of the uterus) can be prevented. Despite this knowledge of over thirty years, there were 345 deaths in 1988, and 1061 new cases. Regular screening, using the Papanicolaou ('Pap') smear, is capable of preventing the development of 99 per cent of this cancer. Screening has been available in all Australian states and territories since the early 1960s. The smear can identify other infections, such as thrush, trichonomas, genital herpes and wart virus.

Australian women are, fortunately, getting the message that the Pap smear is important, for two million have been taken in recent years, out of an estimated target population of 4.8 million women. All women who have ever been sexually active should commence having Pap smears between the ages of eighteen and twenty, or one or two years after the first sexual intercourse, whichever is the latter.

The smears may cease at the age of seventy, for women who have had two normal results within the last five years. On the other hand, women over seventy who have never had a Pap smear, or who ask for one, should be screened.

Prostate cancer

For many men, the great fear is cancer of the prostate gland, which produces most of the fluid in semen. It is the third most common cause of cancer death among Australian men, after lung and colorectal cancer. It is principally but not always a disease among older men. In 1990 one third of the deaths due to prostate cancer in New South Wales occurred in men aged eighty or over. Yet among men with clinical prostate cancer, two-thirds will die from a cause other than this disease.

Controversy continues over the value of screening for prostate cancer, one reason being that women's cancer screening receives priority. The Australian Cancer Society, while declaring it is not insensitive to this fact, nevertheless states there is insufficient evidence that men's health will be advanced through prostate cancer screening. The aim of any screening programme, the Society explains, is not in itself to detect more cancer, nor to reassure people they do not have cancer. The aim, rather, is designed to alter the risks of death from cancer. 'The current state of scientific knowledge suggests that men's objective risk of dying from prostate cancer will not be altered by having any screening test currently available', states the Society, in guidelines prepared for health professionals. A watching brief will nevertheless continue.

> The Australian Cancer Society states there is insufficient evidence that men's health will be advanced through prostate cancer screening.

Non-cancerous enlargement of the prostate can be a problem for men of middle age. A pamphlet prepared by the Australian Health Technology Advisory Committee for the National Health and Medical Research Council titled *What are the Options?* * states that the prostate maintains a constant size from puberty to about 45–50 years of age. At that point, it should begin to decrease progressively in size. For about half or more of men, however, the prostate enlarges instead. The condition is called Benign Prostatic Hyperplasia (BPH). It seems to be a process of age and the normal function of the testes, and has not been associated with any lifestyle or risk factors. The condition can worsen to the point where serious urinary complications may develop, but this is unusual.

The symptoms of BPH include:
- diminution of the calibre and force of the stream of urine
- hesitancy to begin to urinate
- an inability to end the flow abruptly, with dribbling afterwards
- a sensation of incomplete emptying of the bladder.

Accurate diagnosis by a doctor is important, including ruling out prostate cancer. About twenty per cent of men find the condition can be improved, twenty per cent find it gets worse, and the rest find varying severity of the problem. Treatment depends largely on individual men's preferences and circumstances. At the moment, surgery to reduce the prostate – without any open or external incisions – is the main treatment offered.

Several alternative techniques are being evaluated in clinical trials; they include the use of lasers, ultrasound and microwaves to remove the excess tissue, a ballooning device to enlarge the urethra, a stent (artificial tube) to overcome the obstruction and drugs and hormones to reduce the severity of the symptoms as well as the obstruction. All these are still regarded as experimental only, so men should be informed of the status of any alternative offered to them. Other than 'watchful waiting', surgery is still the treatment most confidently recommended by health authorities.

Arthritis – the neglected field

Arthritis has been called the neglected field of medicine. A submission to the Industries Commission Inquiry on the Charitable Sector, by Access Economics Pty Ltd in April 1994, summarised arthritis as 'a frightening scenario'.

> Arthritis has been called the neglected field of medicine.

Here are some of the facts:
- There are over 150 different types of arthritis and related conditions.
- Arthritis is the third most frequent cause of doctor's visits, with some 382 000 visits in the two weeks just before this survey.

> Arthritis is the third most frequent cause of doctor's visits.

- The direct and indirect treatment costs of arthritis and osteoporosis to the Australian community is 5 billion dollars per annum, and equal to one per cent of total gross domestic product.
- Five million Australians, or twenty-nine per cent of the population have musculoskeletal disease. (Arthritis and back trouble were the most commonly reported conditions.)
- Two million Australians, or 12.4 per cent, have arthritis or rheumatism. Of this figure, one million are aged twenty-five to sixty-four years, including 290 000 handicapped by the disease, with 554 273 still in the work force.
- People with arthritis undertake exercise at half the rate of the general population.
- Arthritis has a major impact on lifestyle and family relationships in fifty per cent of cases with those affected. Some sixty per cent of those affected purchase special equipment to modify their homes to assist in normal duties.

The incidence of arthritis and rheumatism is increasing in Australia. The national health surveys of 1977–78 and 1989–90 showed an increase between those dates from 5.7 per cent to 11.5 per cent of the population. The national executive director of the Arthritis Foundation of Australia predicts that if this increase remains constant, then:
- in 2001, 2.5 million will have arthritis, or 12 per cent of the population
- in 2031, 4.2 million will have arthritis, of 16.2 per cent of the population.

These are startling statistics. Government grants do not by any means match the incidence of this disease, for of nearly 60 million dollars dispensed by the National Health and Medical Research Council on competing and continuing grants in 1994, a mere 325 000 dollars, or 0.54 per cent was committed to rheumatology. No wonder Arthritis Foundations work so hard at fund-raising.

By far the more significant aspect of Arthritis Foundations around Australia, however, is their educative role. They have headquarters in every state and territory.* They support research by each contributing to a central pool of funds, which is distributed by the Arthritis Foundation of Australia in the form of research grants. Their literature always takes a positive note, on the theme that 'Something Can be Done!' They organise support groups in metropolitan areas and in country centres and have an army of trained volunteers for their valuable water therapy programmes.

Back pain affects up to eighty per cent of people in Western society, and in Australia it is the third most common cause of absenteeism (after headache and the common cold). Back fitness classes are also run by trained volunteers. Awareness and self-responsibility are important ingredients in functioning with less pain and greater freedom. The Arthritis Foundation also conducts seminars on preventing falls, and workshops on the dozens of ways of managing pain and generally making life easier.

> Awareness and self-responsibility are important ingredients in functioning with less pain and greater freedom.

Their libraries are a constant source of updated, practical information for arthritis and related conditions, and for resource material for researchers. They accentuate the importance of exercise through programmes called 'Exercise Beats Arthritis' and 'Move it or Lose it'.

In practical day-to-day living too, the Arthritis Foundation is a useful source of information on things that help make life easier in and outside the home, and where to get them. These range from helpful gadgets to use in the kitchen and garden, to the most comfortable armchair, a holder for playing cards, or a kneeler for weeding the garden. There are 'don't touch' sensor taps, tap turners for the laundry, therapeutic mattress toppers, shoes for arthritic feet, gloves for arthritic fingers and many more helpful aids.

Arthritis and rheumatism are significant diseases across all age groups, but their prevalence increases with age. Over fifty per cent of people aged 55–64 years, and more than sixty per cent of people aged sixty-five or over, have arthritis or rheumatism. There is radiographic evidence that eighty per cent of people over seventy have arthritis, although not all would be experiencing symptoms.

Creative approaches to exercise are now heartily recommended. The strong message for those with osteoarthritis is that gentle stretching exercise, and regularly moving diseased joints through their full range of motion, is critical in the overall treatment of arthritis conditions. When joints are inflamed, however, rest is needed.

Many positive stories about people with arthritis are regularly reported in *Arthritis Update*, the magazine for members of the Arthritis Foundation in Victoria. Catherine Parsons, a former court reporter taking shorthand at 250 words a minute, developed pain in her neck and shoulders. When she became almost hysterical, she was ordered sick leave. Her advice now is: 'Don't wait until you can't go on. Do something about the pain in the early stages'. Olympic runner Derek Clayton found his knee riddled with osteoarthritis in 1988. Replacement was highly likely, but he proved it was not necessary. He believes this is because his strong muscles and ligaments support the joint. This is easy for him, because he is driven, motivated. As the caption to his story states 'Joints don't like rest'. As a successful competitor in the 1995 Masters Games, Derek is living proof of the value of the Arthritis Foundation's slogan, 'Move it or Lose it'. Marge Watts, six months after a hip replacement, got pain in the thigh region. A general practitioner practising laser acupuncture helped relieve the pain, and Marge is now back to the ballroom dancing that is her favourite pastime.

Gout is one of the most common kinds of arthritis that beset human beings, and contrary to popular belief it is not caused by high living. About 70 000 Australians from all walks of life have the disease, and ninety per cent are men. It arises when there is a build up of uric acid in the body. This is normally dissolved in the bloodstream and passed out through the kidneys. If the body cannot get rid of enough, the build-up will be deposited in the joints, most often in the big toe or the 'bunion' joint and sometimes the elbow or the hand.

Attacks can occur very quickly and unexpectedly and become very painful, but after the first attack, which almost always involves only one joint, it can be months or years before the next one occurs. The Arthritis Foundation advises that one should immediately see a doctor, who will probably prescribe a non-steroidal anti-inflammatory drug which is generally effective within two days. The Foundation also advises that weight control, exercise and diet are all important. Foods such as liver, brains, kidneys, sweetbreads, anchovies, leguminous vegetables, roe, yeast, broths, gravies and sardines can cause increased uric acid levels. So too can more than one glass of wine a day, or one can of beer a day, but otherwise fluid intake is an important factor in controlling gout.

Rheumatoid arthritis is one of the most severe and chronic of rheumatic diseases. It is experienced by about one per cent of the Australian population, mainly those aged 25–50. In its most serious form, it causes painful, badly damaged joints, and can affect other systems of the body. As with other kinds of arthritis, the cause is unknown and no cure has been found. For reasons not fully understood, the body's immune system attacks the tissue surrounding the joint. The chronic inflammation causes joint pain, swelling and stiffness and may eventually lead to deformity of joints. Advances in scientific research, however, assure that proper treatment reduces pain and physical disability. There is also encouraging evidence of the therapeutic value of graded aerobic exercise training for middle-aged to older persons with rheumatoid arthritis.

Professor Ken Muirden, Honorary Medical Director of the Arthritis Foundation of Australia, says one cannot change one's parents, and the environmental triggers that may contribute to its development remain clouded in mystery. Present day therapy is directed at abnormalities in the immune system, in an attempt to stop the disease progressing.

A moving story of one woman's management of rheumatoid arthritis, diagnosed at the age of twenty-six, is told by Loraine Condon. As she states, there is much more to her than arthritis! Her book, *A New Way of Life*,* not only gives practical guidance about managing chronic pain, and techniques for the care of swollen joints; it tells how she has managed to bring up a family and remain a dedicated volunteer community worker, especially in the field of education and the welfare of people with chronic illnesses. Loraine, writes, 'Some days are really awful, others not so bad, and a good day is heaven'.

> How to enjoy a satisfying sex life is another of the issues faced by many people with arthritis.

How to enjoy a satisfying sex life is another of the issues faced by many people with arthritis. The Arthritis Foundation sells a helpful booklet called *Living and Loving* that gives good advice on this.* It is in fact a helpful booklet for all older people. Trying new kinds of intimacy, finding out what is most comfortable, taking turns in giving gentle massage, thoughtful touching, planning sex at a time when one is feeling best, avoiding fatigue, relaxing first in a warm bath all sound like excellent ideas for everyone.

Clearly, the 'missionary' position can be very uncomfortable if the woman has arthritis in the hip joints, or the man has arthritis in the knee, leg or arm joints. Other more comfortable positions are explained, always with the comfort and pleasure of the couple in mind. As the writer of this booklet comments, 'Some people regard sex as a duty, others as a gift. The truth is probably somewhere in between for most of us'.

Diabetes

Diabetes affects around three per cent of the Australian population, but this figure climbs to eleven per cent in the over sixty-five age group. It can develop at any age, but the more common type usually affects people over thirty-five. Diabetes tends to run in families. It is a major cause of blindness and kidney failure. The more weight you carry above the healthy weight range for your age, the higher is your risk of developing diabetes. 'You can't change your age, nor your family history, but you can change your lifestyle', Diabetes Australia claims.

'You can't change your age, nor your family history, but you can change your lifestyle,' Diabetes Australia claims.

Diabetes is a condition in which the body is unable to use properly its main fuel, glucose, a form of sugar. This happens if the pancreas, a gland that lies behind the stomach, is unable to make enough insulin, or the insulin it makes is unable to work effectively. Insulin is a hormone that normally circulates in the blood; it helps glucose to get inside the body's cells. The glucose is then used as a fuel to allow the cells to function normally. Without insulin, or if the body's cells are unresponsive to insulin, glucose cannot enter these cells, but builds up in the blood, spills out into the urine, and, if not treated, can seriously damage the body.

The type commonly affecting older people – non-insulin dependent diabetes mellitus (NIDDM) – is treated by diet and regular exercise, but sometimes tablets also are required. People with diabetes need no special food. Their diet is the same as that recommended for everybody – wholesome foods in balanced amounts. Fruit, vegetables, cereal and bread should form the largest part of the diabetic diet, with plenty of water to drink each day. Fat and sugar should be limited. Foot care is also an important component of a healthy lifestyle for people with diabetes, since poor circulation to the legs can cause gangrene.

The signs that may point to the onset of diabetes, and that need a doctor's attention, are:
- passing urine more often
- feeling thirsty most of the time
- feeling tired or lacking in energy
- feeling hungry more often than usual
- blurred vision
- skin infections and itching.

Once again, this emphasises the necessity for older people to have regular check-ups, as a matter of course.

Diabetes Australia* has offices in every capital city, and in many regional centres. It administers the Commonwealth funded National Diabetic Supplies Scheme which provides significant benefits for people with diabetes. Beneficiaries (who register through any Diabetes Australia office) gain concessions on insulin syringes, needles, and urine and blood glucose testing strips. Diabetes Australia also plays an important educational role in arranging discussion and support groups and providing literature.

In short ...

1 Many cancers can be attributed to lifestyle or environmental factors, and could be prevented. Results of research are freely available – the rest is common sense.

2 Early detection is another important factor in cancer treatment. Screening programmes are there for our protection, and reassurance.

3 Educating ourselves about signs and symptoms is yet another means of dealing with the possibility of cancer, and early treatment.

4 Education is also important in the management of arthritis, and in the day-to-day living with the condition in its different forms.

5 Changing one's lifestyle is an important way of dealing with late-onset diabetes.

6 If we inform and educate ourselves, and then act on what we know, we can each have some control over our health, despite the gloomy picture painted by the statisticians.

9
Planning the future down on the farm

The needs of older people in rural Australia are both the same as, and different from, those in urban areas. For all of us, the level of our involvement in our work, done perhaps over a lifetime, will some day be less than it is now. When an agricultural researcher casually remarked 'farmers never retire', I realised this was a major difference. For many farming families, the business that maintains them is also home.

> For many farming families, the business that maintains them is also home.

Australia may be one of the most urbanised countries in the world, with eighty per cent of the population living on three per cent of the land mass, but the other twenty per cent are of vital importance to our history, our economy, our future and our sense of ourselves as a nation. There are about 130 000 farming units in Australia and ninety per cent of them are owned by families. The non-metropolitan community of this country represents thirty per cent of the nation's workforce, with agriculture and mining producing eighty-two per cent of the country's exports. Many people not on farms consider themselves to be more country than city oriented and the word 'rural' in the context of this chapter refers to anything outside the capital cities.

Drought, floods, bush fires, enormous economic crises and unprecedented structural adjustments have not been the only problems experienced by the farming community. As parents get older and children leave home, often forever, the question arises across thousands of rural households – what next? It is a crucial issue for today's farming community, as it is for older people everywhere who have given their lives to a family business. The average age of Australian farmers is fifty-four. Most of their farms cannot be split any further, and with farm incomes declining, many properties struggle to provide one income, let alone two. Even when a member of the younger generation is interested in taking over from parents ready to take a rest, he or she seldom has the finance to buy out the share due to other siblings.

> The average age of Australian farmers is fifty-four.

Transferring the family farm

One of the key – and more complicated – issues to be considered in the transfer of the family farm is stamp duty. There are certain exemptions available in New South Wales, Victoria, Queensland, South Australia and Western Australia.

With these problems in mind, one imaginative farm adviser got together a group to write a booklet, *Transferring the Family Farm*,* which was published by the Department of Agriculture in 1991. The work that motivated this book was a first, and acted as a catalyst for broader activity.

There followed, for example, a manual for farm transfer planning entitled *Your Farm, Their Future – Together** and based on research carried out at the University of Western Sydney, Hawkesbury, and funded by the Rural Industries Research and Development Corporation. Yanco College in New South Wales also produced a significant paper entitled 'Retirement and Estate Planning for Rural Families'.*

Bill Thompson, a solicitor with expertise in farm transfer, joined with a farm financial consultant, Peter Talty, to produce a kit, 'Handing on the Family Farm: Let's get Started',* which assists families to begin the process, reduce the cost and encourage discussion within the farm family. Sample letters that must be written to appropriate institutions such as banks and insurance companies, a family questionnaire that softens the difficulties in expressing thoughts and aspirations, and a record sheet to keep track of progress, are all part of this useful guide.

A video, 'Let's Talk',* shows the life of a typical farm family, and looks at issues of self-esteem, levels of communication and handling conflict. Lyn Sykes, a Dubbo-based Family Life counsellor, plays herself as the mediator for a family meeting, a role she has taken on for many farm families. Lyn stresses that without family meetings it is too easy for people to change the subject, or simply leave the room if they do not want to talk about the issues. As she says, there are no textbook answers, for every family has its unique scenario and must develop its own creative solutions to its problems.

The Law Institute and the Institute of Chartered Accountants, with offices in all capital cities, now provide assistance in planning the future of the family farm.

As stated in the book, *Transferring the Family Farm*, business partners are often close relatives and it is difficult to make hard-nosed decisions when they affect your family. Likewise, important family lifestyle decisions tend to be deferred or avoided if they interfere with the running of the farm. Yet it is crucial that farming families talk about the future because of the very ties that bind business to family life. The cost of continuing to avoid discussion may mean frustration and even greater

> Business partners are often close relatives and it is difficult to make hard-nosed decisions when they affect your family.

deterioration of family relationships. The challenge is to find a solution that will be good for the farm as a business, and good for the family. Most families would like to aim for a solution that allows the family relationship to continue in a healthy spirit of understanding and co-operation.

One of the book's many strong points is its advice on how to get started in what must be a business, rather than a social, occasion. A good way to begin is to have everyone describe what they would, ideally, like to see happen with the farm. During the discussion, which should continue to be frank and open, ground rules are helpful, such as no interruptions, and sticking to the subject without getting side-tracked. Listening is vital. No-one should expect a solution out of the first meeting, so arrangements should be made for further talks, at times convenient for everybody. (Many townspeople could benefit from such advice!)

The big issue, of 'who gets what and when?' must be understood and supported by the family. If any member is not taken into account, or left uncertain, difficulties will follow. 'What is fair' needs to be established early, and accepted by all. Fair does not necessarily mean equal.

People need to express their fears. As the book states, the wife and mother may fear that her husband will drive himself to an early grave by hard work, and that she will be left alone to cope with being dependent on a son and daughter-in-law. The second son, who has worked on the family farm for the past ten years, may fear that his elder brother, who has shown little interest over the years, will inherit most of the farm. The parents may watch a rocky marriage between their daughter and son-in-law and worry that divorce could lead to his 'taking' the farm.

Working with professional advisers – a theme that runs throughout *Life Begins at Fifty-something* – makes good sense, especially in obtaining the full range of financial or legal options available to members of a family business. Just as this writer has sought advice in the preparation of this chapter from people well versed in rural affairs (and especially from the book *Transferring the*

Farm) so too will specialists be able to answer major questions like the following:
- How and when should the management of the farm be passed on to the next generation?
- Do you want to try to keep the farm viable for the next generation?
- How and when should the family assets, including the farm, be distributed?
- Who should receive the assets?

All these questions have legal, financial and farm management implications.

Once all family members have had their say, the decisions reached can be treated as an agreement. If the family situation changes due to a death or marriage, it would be sensible to review the agreement and possibly renegotiate parts of it. *Transferring the Farm* offers useful principles to consider when making such decisions, and again they are eminently helpful for all families, in city and country alike. The principles are:
- Attempt to divide the assets fairly if not equally.
- Try to keep things as simple as possible.
- The security, independence and satisfaction of all people involved is very important.
- It is not unreasonable to expect children to pay for a share of the assets (for example, to buy into the farm with their share of the income).
- Sons and daughters have equal rights.
- People should not be frightened to spend money obtaining appropriate professional advice.
- The timing of the handover of management should be clearly indicated.
- Decisions should be flexible for changing circumstances.
- Beneficiaries should know what to expect so that they can plan their lives accordingly.
- Be careful about making loans to family members. Conflict

arises easily when favourable loans are given out at the expense of other children.
- Selling the family property and dividing the proceeds may be a sensible option in some situations.

In sum, communication is all important. This may be a truism, but it is the only way forward, if a healthy spirit of understanding and co-operation is to prevail.

Legal issues for farm women

The feminist lawyer, Dr Jocelynne Scutt, has for almost twenty years been making public her concerns about the role of women as business partners and business wives. These concerns relate particularly to rural women. She sees the law, where women are both wives and partners, in a state of flux. There remains an assumption firmly fixed in the psyche, she argues, that paid work is 'more valuable' than unpaid work, and that the paid work men do is 'more valuable' than the paid work women do. She also sees a tendency in judges to presuppose certain changes in society that favour male litigants – that is, that men are participating equally with women in unpaid work in the home – when there is no research available that supports this notion at all, and indeed the opposite appears to be the case.

Jocelynne Scutt sees further problems in the case of the farm. There is a tendency, she states, for business assets, including farms, to be seen as the product of the work of the male partner, not the female partner. If there is any acknowledgement of a wife's contribution to business assets, including farms, 'it's one that downgrades that contribution and does not see it as equal to that of the husband'. Contrarily, if the business asset, including the farm, is in the wife's name, the tendency is to inflate the husband's contribution to it. That is, men are seen as the major contributors to business assets (including farms), or the primary builders of such assets. Women, Jocelynne Scutt argues, tend to be seen as 'helpers' or 'assistants' or 'supporters', not as equal business partners or equal farmers.

In her workshop, entitled 'Who Gets the Farm?' at the Women and Farms Gathering at Glenormiston in April 1994, Jocelynne Scutt spoke about 'sexually transmitted debt'. (This is a phrase coined by the Women and Credit Group.) Many times a woman may be asked to 'sign on the dotted line'. Signing can mean that the farm is 'handed over' to the bank or finance company. Too many women, she stated, are caught in situations where they sign, not knowing what they are signing, or thinking 'it's for the best', believing it is the best way of dealing with loans and financial problems.

Sometimes women sign because they are threatened physically or emotionally. It is vital that women do understand the legal consequences of signing documents, whether a mortgage, company documents, or loan papers. It is equally vital that women recognise their own responsibilities where finances are concerned, as well as making sure they are not held responsible for debts that are not properly attributed to them.

> It is vital that women do understand the legal consequences of signing documents, whether a mortgage, company documents, or loan papers.

Other issues canvassed at that workshop that are of general concern were inheritance, separation and divorce. Is an older woman, formerly wife and still mother of the son who inherits the farm, obliged to live out the rest of her days as a 'burden' to the household, when her deceased husband's will hands the farm over to the children? Is there a need to ensure that a woman's work is recognised in a concrete way, so that the farm is not simply willed away, by her husband, without her having any say?

The *Family Law Act 1975* recognises that unpaid work by women in the home, maintenance of the family home, caring for husband and children, is valuable. It recognises that this work contributes to the accumulation of marital assets. The work that women do on the farm, in addition to home-making, such as milking, feeding the shearers, cropping, cropdusting and sheep-dipping should be recognised as asset-producing when the Family Court of Australia considers the distribution of assets at a time of separation and divorce. As Jocelynne Scutt declares, women's voices must be heard on these matters. Their rights on paper must be translated into rights in practice.

The 'silly old bugger syndrome'

It is widely acknowledged that men involved in farming are less willing to consider change, and less willing to be motivators for change. Solicitor Bill Thompson has observed that older farming men are reluctant to discuss plans for the future, on the basis that *their* fathers did not discuss the future with them. Whether it was the share of the farm, passing it on to heirs, or even the details of wills, these issues have too often been taboo subjects. The patriarchal system has been entrenched for so long!

> Men involved in farming are less willing to consider change, and less willing to be motivators for change. The patriarchal system has been entrenched for so long!

Even farm advisers, leaders of farmer organisations and employees of companies supplying farm equipment have been male, with a few recent exceptions like Mrs Heather Mitchell, former president of the Victorian Farmers Federation and now (at the age of seventy-seven) president of the Public Land Council and deputy chair of the *Young* Farmers Finance Council of Australia.

Bill Thompson states:

> I call it 'the silly old bugger syndrome'. I often find that wives will say that they know their husbands do wish to discuss the issue, but always they find an excuse not to do so. To get around this problem I often agree to meet families on their farms, and

then the issue cannot be avoided. Once the ice is broken, discussions can generally be productive. It can take anywhere between a number of weeks and eighteen months to work through the issues.

The major problem is the male ethos or ego. Bill Thompson finds that older farming women and younger farmers, whether male or female, are keen to discuss and work through problems, and as a result the older males have to be prompted to participate. He often quotes 'The Farmer's Will' when speaking at seminars on transfer of the family farm. While it reveals a great deal about the negativity of older farmers, it also reveals a cry for help.

I leave –

To my Wife: My overdraft – maybe she can explain it.

To my Son: Equity on my car – now he'll have to work to meet the repayments.

To my Banker: My soul – he's got a mortgage on it anyway.

To my Neighbour: My clown suit – he will need it if he continues to farm as he has in the past.

To the Rural Adjustment Board: My unpaid bills – they took some real chances on me and I want to do the same for them.

To the Australian Wheat Board: My remaining wheat pool equity – they'll need it to pay the wharfies' exorbitant pay rates.

To my Farm Advisor: My farm plan – maybe he can understand it.

To the Local Shire Council: My pile of discarded shock absorbers and blown tyres – I suggest they make appropriate reduction on my overdue rates.

To the Junk Man: My machinery – he's had his eyes on it for years.

To my Undertakers: A special request – six implements and fertiliser dealers – four pall bearers please – they are used to carrying me.

To my Weatherman: Rain, sleet and hail for the funeral please – no sense in having nice weather now.

To the Grave Digger: Don't bother! The hole I am in should be big enough.

The Monument Maker: Carve an epitaph, something like this:

> Under the stone a farmer lies
> No-one laughs and no-one cries
> Where he has gone and how he fares
> No-one knows and no-one cares.

Alternatively, if I am cremated send the ashes to the Taxation Department with a brief note reading: '**There you are bastards! Now you've got the lot.**'

The loss of self-esteem and purpose in this desolate statement needs careful consideration. Thankfully, some work has been done, and continues to be done with male farmers alone, and with them and their families. A group of academics from the University of Western Sydney/Hawkesbury, Macquarie University and the University of New South Wales undertook a major survey that, among other issues, considered generational change on the farm. They ran twenty-five workshops for over 2500 older farmers and their wives, to consider what issues were affecting them most as they moved through different stages of life (and a further fifty workshops for younger farmers).

The outcome was a major report, 'The Transfer of the Family Farm Business in a Changing Rural Society'.* It emphasised lack of communication; the transfer of the farm was in fact taking place in silence. It found that in practice, farm transfer was too often seen as an event, rather than a gradual (paternalistic) process, in which lawyers and accountants are the principal advisers. The potential for conflict was often greater when two generations were farming together, and both generations were living off it.

> The potential for conflict was often greater when two generations were farming together.

The workshops revealed that forty-two per cent of the older (first) generation of male farmers had not spoken to their spouse about the future of the farm, and its transfer to the younger generation. Sixty-three per cent of the first generation had not spoken about this with their 'returned' child, even though this child might have been home for up to thirty years. Eighty-four per cent of the first generation had not included their daughter-in-law in any discussion on farm transfer. The added complexity of the daughter-in-law, who is usually affected by any transfer decisions made, tended to increase the silence of the parents. Of the second generation, sixty per cent indicated no discussion had taken place with their spouse.

The father who often held the land titles felt the area of farm transfer was his primary responsibility, yet he was not the one initiating the discussions. Dennis Gamble, one of the academics from the University of Western Sydney/Hawkesbury involved in the project, offered the following reasons for the father not being able to talk about it:

- It was too hard for Dad to work it all out; how to keep a viable farm for the returning generation, to be fair to the other children and how to secure their own retirement with not enough assets to achieve all this.
- Dad does not know how to begin to talk about it, while Mum has the people skills but does not generally own the farm titles.
- It is too hard for Dad to let his life's work and future security pass to the next generation. Older parents also fear the prospect of divorce in the younger generation, and the resulting loss of the farm if they hand ownership over to them.
- Dad wants to keep waiting to see how things turn out … which child shows interest, what sort of spouse the younger returning generation marries, the stability of the marriage, and how the grandchildren turn out.
- Dad and Mum wonder how to treat fairly the children who do not return home to the farm. They know that passing it on to their son invariably means the exclusion or partial exclusion of other children from the farm asset.

The juggling act and its associated problems are further revealed in this generalisation, based upon the farm families interviewed:

Finally they [Dad and Mum] are thinking about their retirement and security. They have no off-farm investments or outside income sources, so they are dependent on the farm asset for all their future needs. Therefore they are worrying about the possible loss of the farm in the event of the break-up of their son's marriage. They have also held back on giving their son financial or decision-making responsibility in case his decisions put their life's work at risk. For these reasons they have not handed over the farm ownership.

Here is the acknowledged anguish of one father:

I have been so long at the helm now I have a bit of trepidation passing it on. The decision is hard because it is final, nobody is responsible for it but yourself. I have tried to dodge behind a tree regarding this situation.

Some families have begun to develop a shared understanding of one another's concerns and future intentions, since taking part in the farm transfer workshops. They have found the following to be of benefit (and much of this would be of benefit to all families, irrespective of where they live):

> Some families have begun to develop a shared understanding of one another's concerns and future intentions, since taking part in the farm transfer workshops.

- wills updated
- agreement on the time frame for retirement, for the shared arrangements for income and costs of transferring of the land titles
- enduring power of attorney instigated to cover the principal members of the family
- agreement as to what would be fair to all children
- documentation of family loans and agreements
- overall strategy for two generations farming together involving an increase in farm production through a farm development plan.

Networks for women across rural Australia

There are now two million women in rural and remote Australia, and they are a vital, integral part of the agricultural sector. Over 80 000 of these women are working as farmers, farm managers or farm labourers. In the *National Farmers Magazine* in 1985, it was estimated that women contributed approximately 5 billion dollars to the Australian rural economy. This was a lot more than making scones and jam! Although the number of women who successfully run farms is growing, the perception remains that farming is man's work – especially in the banking industry.

All the more reason therefore to honour the Australian Broadcasting Commission's annual Rural Woman of the Year Awards. The national winner in 1995 was Robyn Tredwell, from the Kimberleys in Western Australia. The NSW winner was a mature-age small farm operator from the Scone district of the Upper Hunter in New South Wales, Beverlee Adams. Beverlee had her farm declared a wild life sanctuary in 1973, in the belief that grazing and wild life preservation can be combined.

Communication is the key to a dynamic process occurring in country life around Australia, through the rural women's movement. In 1986, two lively women active in rural and community affairs, Jenni Mitchell and Anna Lottkowitz, were employed by the Victorian government to develop the Rural Women's Network (RWN). The Network was born with two major objectives. The first was to link women's groups and interested individuals into a network towards sharing resources and skills to meet the needs of rural women. The second was to enable women in rural Victoria, through their own contact and support network, to have a more active and influential role in government decisions that affect their lives and those of their families and communities. In particular,

> Communication is the key to a dynamic process occurring in country life around Australia, through the rural women's movement.

the Network was created to facilitate change in the status of rural women. RWN Victoria circulates a free newsletter, *Network*.*

In New South Wales, the first Rural Women's Conference at Parkes in 1991 demanded state government funding to establish a programme similar to RWN Victoria. Its newsletter is *The Country Web*.*

In 1992, RWN NSW worked with St Vincent's Sisters of Charity to establish Country Care Link, a confidential information, counselling and referral service for rural New South Wales. RWN has developed a centre for access to resources on rural women and rural communities. It supports women's health and information forums across the state, updates and distributes the NSW Country Guide Directory of government services. Women come together for the annual Women of the Land Gatherings now held in a different region each year.

RWN NSW produced a special drought edition of its newsletter late in 1994. It covered a whole range of issues, from taking care of the stock to taking care of one's self in this time of acute stress. Drought initiatives by organisations and agencies showed how those suffering hardship in the rural downturn could be supported in practical, monetary and other ways. This edition of the newsletter remains a significant drought resource for all rural families. On the initiative of RWN, NSW Agriculture also produced a video as a special resource for drought support, *Let's Talk*.*

Other states are following Victoria and New South Wales. Although not necessarily functioning in precisely similar ways, all have common goals in linking rural women, and with the wellbeing of women always the priority. Moves are under way to create state-funded networks in both Western and South Australia.* As the president of Queensland Rural Women Inc.* has stated, women in Australia are coming together to shake the invisibility many feel in their rural communities.

There have been, and still are, enormous contributions made by, and for, rural women and their families through the Country Women's Association.* Founded in New South Wales in 1922, the

CWA now has about 51 000 members across the country, and covers issues of fundamental concern to rural families. Entirely voluntary, it is one of the most highly regarded lobby groups in Australia. It has been the training ground for many outstanding women leaders, and also been the springboard for many other important community activities.

Of current concern to CWA members are the major matters of closure of health services in country areas, domestic violence, accidents on farms (especially on tractors), and caring for carers in isolated areas. Mrs Joy Ambrose of Ararat represented the CWA on the Victorian Consumers Forum for the Aged. With a near-blind mother of eighty-five whose dementia was becoming apparent, and a forty-nine-year-old husband forced out of work by a massive heart attack, Joy Ambrose knew at first hand the enormous burden of continuous caring. She helped press for the formation of carers associations in Victoria and Tasmania – then the only Australian states without them – and was elected the first president of the Carers Association in Victoria. She and her organisation continue to press for more government funding, for respite care *within the family home*. Both carer and cared-for need to remain in familiar surroundings to feel secure.

Australia took a lead in organising and hosting the first International Conference for Women in Agriculture, in Melbourne in July 1994. Over 850 participated, with over 100 overseas women representing thirty-four countries. Most delegates were of mature age, although their ages ranged from nineteen to eighty years! The bonding force was their great love of the land and agriculture. Six key areas evolved: education, visibility and recognition, decision-making and participation, networking, environmental sustainability, and social justice. Six 'Vision' statements see women participating fully in all aspects of the rural sector, with networks operating for women's equal participation in developing and developed countries.

> Most delegates were of mature age. The bonding force was their great love of the land and agriculture.

Following the international conference, the first National Rural Women's Forum was held in Canberra in June 1995. The forum welcomed the establishment of a rural women's unit in the Federal government. The initiative for this unit grew out of lobbying by the leaders in the rural women's movement.

Australian Women in Agriculture (AWiA) is primarily a grass-roots farmer organisation, with a membership from all parts of the continent, covering all occupations dealing with the agricultural industry. There are lawyers, university lecturers, secretaries, government workers, full-time mothers, wives, scientists, vets and researchers, through to journalists, bankers, members of parliament, as well as a broad range of farmers. The national committee of nine members meets once a month by telephone link up, and face to face when possible. Since most farm women spend the decades in their twenties and thirties 'mothering, wifeing and farming', it is often only in their mid to late forties that they can branch out into extended community activity. Many members of AWiA are therefore over fifty. Yet they recognise the need to include younger women, not only by providing child care and other forms of support, but to encourage them into future leadership roles. Their newsletter, *The Buzz*,* is fertile with ideas, a hive of activity, and all about cross-fertilisation: bees getting their messages to each other!

The latest development is the Foundation for Australian Agricultural Women (FAAW),* an independent, non-political, national, philanthropic organisation with a mission to support and advance agricultural women for the benefit of all Australians. FAAW has established advisory groups to work closely with the Australia-wide board of directors in four distinct areas: social justice; education and training; legal, finance management and decision-making; health and safety.

Audrey Hardman of Mandurama, New South Wales, is an outstanding example of what this book is about, reaching her fullest potential in her middle years, and still planning to do big things in the future, always with a view to making services, conditions and opportunities better for rural Australians. Her central focus is Bradgate Park, the property she has worked with her husband Gerald since their marriage in 1959. Mother and grandmother, she has been company secretary, director, book-keeper, and general farmhand, while being deeply involved in rural and community life at local, regional, state and federal levels. She has been a tennis coach, director of the local hotel, partner in a fashion boutique, and among her interests lists music, art, floral art, swimming, gardening, interior decorating, crafts and cooking.

Audrey Hardman is an influential bridge between the entirely voluntary Country Women's Association and the new government-funded project of the 1990s, the Rural Women's Network. She has strong involvement in both. She has taken a higher profile in the TAFE sector, first as a member of the Western Institute TAFE Council, and chair in 1995. She believes TAFE has provided a most valuable service to rural Australia; it has enormous potential to deliver appropriate, more flexible, mixed-mode courses to meet future needs.

*The Rural Book** is an annual resource guide to the range of major services and programmes provided by twenty-six Commonwealth departments and agencies. It brings together information on such widely ranging topics as health and safety, housing, help for people in business, tourism, assistance for primary producers, taxation, transport and travel, programmes to support migrants, Aboriginal people and other specific groups, and dealing with government departments. The address and telephone number of every rural counselling service throughout Australia is but one of its many resources. It is free and post-free to country people.

Countrylink,* the Commonwealth government's information access service for country people, travels around Australia with a shopfront service at selected agricultural shows and field days, offering and gathering information by talking to people about their needs. It also provides a video lending library.

Finally, there is a great deal of good sense for all people, no matter where they live, in '20 Clues to Rural Community Survival' which *The Country Web* published in its winter edition, 1995. The clues come from the United States, but may be regarded as of universal significance. To survive, we need:

- evidence of community pride
- emphasis on quality in business and community life
- willingness to invest in the future
- participatory approach to decision-making
- co-operative community spirit
- realistic appraisal of future opportunities
- awareness of competitive positioning
- knowledge of the physical environment
- active economic development programmes
- deliberate transition of power to a younger generation of leaders
- acceptance of women in leadership roles
- strong belief in and support for education
- problem-solving approach to providing health care
- strong multi-generational family orientation
- strong presence of traditional institutions that are integral to community life
- attention to sound and well-maintained infrastructure
- careful use of fiscal resources
- sophisticated use of information resources
- willingness to seek help from the outside
- conviction that in the long run, you have to do it yourself.

A significant national rural conference on ageing, 'Rewriting the Future', was organised by Sturt University's Faculty of Health Studies and held at the Albury campus in September 1995. It covered an array of topics, such as exercise for older people and home care, farm injuries to persons over sixty, aged care in different settings, preventing abuse of older people, ethnicity, ageing and learning, community theatre, hydrotherapy and pain management.

One session was devoted to lesbians over sixty years of age in rural settings; they were described as 'a triply invisible group – old, women and lesbians'. Their ability to live positive, productive and happy lives was seen to be remarkable, given the degree of discrimination they have been exposed to during their life-time. This achievement was described as a sociological phenomenon in itself.

The conference convenor, Celia Saw, undertook on behalf of Sturt University to establish a unit through which ongoing seminars and conferences would continue the debate on rural issues and ageing. She presented a paper at the Albury conference, looking at older women in rural businesses. All the women in her study had juggled multiple roles of home, farm and community work. Living in the same community, they remained separate in their personal struggles. The case studies made visible the valuable work of rural older women, and their courageous struggle to combine personal growth with home and business life.

'Their efforts are undervalued', Celia Saw claimed, 'particularly their achievements for change in the wider rural community'. She was particularly concerned that rural linkages for older women will remain under-developed unless more knowledge is acquired to ascertain what they need to appropriately negotiate their ageing. 'These women have been the mainstay of social, economic, educational and cultural life', she added. 'It would repay them in some way if they were personally and collectively assisted to achieve social justice, through new forms of social structure and community organisation to which they can relate.'

> Rural linkages for older women will remain under-developed unless more knowledge is acquired to ascertain what they need to appropriately negotiate their ageing.

A keynote speaker at Albury, Dr Sara Arber from Britain, emphasised that the voices of older people themselves must be heard, 'letting them define issues of concern, rather than imposing the ageist concerns of social scientists'. For too long older people have been conceptualised as a burden on society and family members, and primarily studied within a range of social problems, from poverty to ill-health and disability.

Dr Arber quoted a Canadian researcher, whose view surely rings true for Australians also:

> Three sets of factors intertwine to make the role of older women increasingly important in the future. First is our growing numerical strength with its potential political power. Second is the struggle experienced by many older women against poverty, institutionalisation, and the combined effects of ageism and sexism. Third is the gender-structured positions held by women in our society, which teach us to care and connect with others in both perception and action.

In short ...

1 Retirement for farming families is made more complex by the fact that their business is also their home.

2 When business partners are also members of the family, business decisions of necessity will have an impact on the family, and vice versa.

3 Family meetings to discuss issues and make decisions should, ideally, be business orientated, making it difficult for members to change the subject or simply leave the room.

4 The cost of avoiding discussion can lead to general frustration and relationships can deteriorate.

5 Ground rules are useful and listening is essential.

6 Discussion must be frank and open so that everyone can voice their individual concerns, and even fears.

7 Professional advisers – financial and/or legal – can answer questions and act as mediators.

8 Women's views and needs must be addressed. Women should be regarded as equal partners according to their contributions.

9 The paternalistic system surrounding farming has meant that women have been excluded from decision-making for generations, even when the decisions have directly affected them.

10 There are rural networks existing to enhance women's communications throughout Australia, waiting to be utilised and enjoyed.

10

Repartnering in the nineties

One cannot move through a review of what is occurring at the age of fifty-something without acknowledging the issues of marriage, divorce and, that word, repartnering.

The second time around – or even the first

There are many premarriage courses available for couples. From all I have seen of their literature, they seem eminently worthwhile, with trained counsellors offering advice and support in congenial surroundings. For the age group to whom this book is directed, 'marriage preparation' might appear to be far too late, for many of those nearing fifty will have been in marriage or a relationship for many years.

On the other hand, it is never too late to seek advice. People in trouble have always received all kinds of well-meant advice, especially from other family members and friends. Added to traditional sources of advice has been the emergence in this century of trained counsellors. In the United States as early as the late 1920s, in the United Kingdom in the late 1930s, and in

Australia in the late 1940s there gradually developed a more rational approach to the whole business of helping people, notably with marital problems.

Counselling practices were constantly tested, and the disciplines of psychology, religion, medicine, sociology and education were all brought to bear on the notion of healing. Rather than give advice, the healer co-operates with a willing client. Clients, without coercion or interference, are offered a service whereby they are enabled to help themselves.

> Rather than give advice, the healer co-operates with a willing client.

Marriage Guidance Councils were established throughout Australia. One of the founders in Victoria, Dr W. L. Carrington, was often heard to speak about the 'the healing of marriage'. In counselling for both marriage preparation and parenthood in practical and constructive discussion, he would have a general question always in the foreground. It was a question worth remembering: 'What can you offer toward a better partnership, irrespective of your partner?'

Anglican Marriage Education and Counselling Service (AMECS)* is a highly respected non-profit agency approved by the Federal Attorney-General's Department to conduct programmes under the provisions of the Family Law Act. This means clients, regardless of their religious, social, cultural or economic circumstances, are assured of the highest professional standards of training and practice.

AMECS runs specific courses for people planning to remarry, including the question of stepchildren, as well as marriage enrichment courses. The success of all of them depends on the participants' willingness to respond fully and honestly. Experience has shown that they gain most value by completing the remarriage course at least three months before their wedding. Topics covered over three evenings include communication, conflict resolution, relationship expectations, sexuality and intimacy, value systems, and the influence of the birth family, or family of origin. Religious aspects of the preparation are left to the celebrant, although spiritual issues can be discussed by arrangement.

Each Catholic diocese, through the local welfare agency Centacare,* provides a marriage education programme. Many Centacare agencies utilise an inventory devised in the United States, FOCCUS, to facilitate open couple communication, understanding and study. FOCCUS poses specific questions for couples to examine together before entering a second marriage. The questions that follow are explored by participating couples, and are relevant to our subject group. They are planned to see where each person is, both in relation to the previous marriage and in helping meet their expectations of the next marriage.

- What feelings have we shared with each other surrounding the care of our children?
- How will memories of my previous partner affect our new marriage?
- Does my partner's previous sexual relationship cause me concern?
- Have we agreed on the way we will furnish our new home? What possessions will we bring?
- Is it OK for my spouse to discipline the children?
- Have we talked over enough issues with our children?

Relationships Australia (WA) Inc (formerly Marriage Guidance Western Australia) is a further source. 'Working Together' comprises six pamphlets guiding couples through common pitfalls. One is titled 'Two Persons/One Relationship'; another is 'Second Chance'.

At present, about one-third of all Australian marriages are second marriages. The Australian Bureau of Statistics reported 45 665 divorces granted in 1992, the highest annual figure since the record year of 1976 when the *Family Law Act* came into effect and introduced no-fault divorce. Although divorce rates continue to be high with about forty-three per cent of marriages ending in separation within thirty years, and second marriages breaking down at an even higher rate, marriage remains an attractive option. The search for happiness is certainly a great motivator, yet it is usually a by-product of what we are and do.

> Marriage remains an attractive option. The search for happiness is certainly a great motivator, yet it is usually a by-product of what we are and do.

Some couples, having shed the constraints of youth, say they only reach their sexual prime in mature age (from 35–55 years), and this often means during a second or later partnership. Dr David Schnarch of Colorado, when the guest of Relationships Australia Inc.* (formerly Marriage Guidance) late in 1995, was quoted often in the media for advocating 'orgasm with your eyes open'. He stressed that most people do not reach their full sexual capacity, and those who do are usually in 'their fourth, fifth and sixth decade'.

Professor Patricia Noller and a colleague, Dr Victor Callan, in their book *Marriage and the Family*,* show how levels of individualism have risen as sex role beliefs have changed. Individuals are seeking more satisfaction from relationships. Partners are striving to become equal partners. Everything is now open to negotiation, and new marriages are being built upon agreements for equity and role flexibility.

As Callan and Noller state, these ideals are placing new pressures on marriages. Individuals, while expecting a greater balance and sharing in the costs of marriage, also expect far greater personal rewards. When partners fail to agree on what is equitable, and a partner is unwilling to enter into negotiation and change, the marriage is likely to end. The inflexibility of husbands in relation to working wives is seen as a basic problem. Working wives expect more role flexibility from their husbands. Yet according to Callan and Noller, most research shows that there is little difference in husbands' contribution to housework between those whose wives work, and those whose wives do not work.

The possibility of a 'sleeping partner' or, as they call it, an alternative partner, is apparently more anticipated than real. Studies of divorcing couples show that the majority do not have an alternative partner to help make the planned break-up a reality.

The reasons given for seeking a divorce differ. Husbands list in-laws and sexual incompatibility more than wives do. Wives emphasise financial problems, verbal and physical abuse, excessive drinking, lack of love and mental cruelty. Lack of common interests, lack of communication and husbands' long absences are often mentioned.

Because many of these causes are long-term, it has been found that the decision to separate is the end of a process that has developed over a period. 'Things have been going bad for a long time' is an oft-quoted reason given at the time of separation. Women have been shown to consider separation at an earlier stage than men.

The stepfamily

Dr Ruth Webber is senior lecturer in sociology at Australian Catholic University. She is known throughout the country, not only in academia but in talk-back radio, for her wise counsel on step-parenting. She runs educational programmes in every Australian state and territory for those living in stepfamilies, and has done similar work in Canada.

Two editions of Ruth Webber's book, *Living in a Stepfamily*,* have sold well because they offer sound advice on what works, especially in surviving the adolescent members of newly created families. There is also a leader's handbook for use in groups, and a video for those step-parents not accustomed to reading. Her research has shown that stepfamilies can be exciting, rewarding and a great deal of fun. Overall, her advice to step-parents is 'Don't be afraid — grab hold of the problems that

> Research has shown that stepfamilies can be exciting, rewarding and a great deal of fun.

confront you'. As she states: 'There is no doubt that stepfamilies encounter many difficulties. However, like all families, stepfamilies have low points and stressful times, but like other family types, there are also times that are happy.'

Her chapters end with a series of 'things to think about', many of which any family would find well worth considering. On relationships with children, for example, here are some of Ruth Webber's suggestions:

- If children are rude or insolent, you ought to tell them quite firmly that such behaviour is unacceptable.
- Stress for the couple may be reduced if they can discuss and agree upon an appropriate joint discipline policy for the household.
- Access children are in one sense visitors, and in another residents. The couple should be wary that they don't become unwitting accomplices in the children's endeavour to establish an 'in' and an 'out' group in the family.
- Life is pleasanter for children if both of the natural parents refrain from showing their jealousy and anger.
- Don't blame yourself for all the children's problems.

As Ruth Webber states, any relationship requires hard and painful work. Step-parents do not have the luxury of getting to know their stepchildren in a tension-free environment. The stepchildren may be hostile or suspicious towards the step-parent and they may have preconceived ideas about what the step-parent is like. Trust, acceptance and respect will come slowly and will have to be earned. There will be many set-backs and an innocent or thoughtless remark can set the relationship back.

It is easy to become discouraged, and for this reason step-parents will feel less despondent by not expecting too much too soon. They should try to take pleasure even in the smallest token of acceptance from the stepchildren. Above all, it is important to prevent resentment from festering, so openness with one's partner is all important.

According to Ruth Webber, there are two basic types of roles that seem to lead to satisfying relationships between a step-parent and a stepchild. She calls one the *parent-like* step-parent. This role may be adopted when entering a family where the children are young, and it can be a warm, affectionate and nurturing role, with discipline and control accepted as the children grow older. In some cases the stepchild prefers the company of the step-parent, and is able to confide more openly than with the parent.

The second type of step-parent role that fits into a positive category she calls the *friend-like* role. Generally, step-parents who play this role do not try to exercise much control over stepchildren, preferring to leave this to the parent. In such cases it is crucial for the parent to carry out the responsibility for discipline, with both parent and step-parent being clear about the roles each wants to play. Warmth is often reciprocated in this type of stepfamily, for the two generations are like friends, living rather as compatible flatmates, or the young person seeing the older as an aunt or uncle.

Children are aware of their power to make trouble in a stepfamily, and some researchers believe the child is more influential in changing the step-parent's behaviour than the other way around. Only if the step-parent continues to show an interest in the life of the stepchild, and avoids becoming involved in control issues, can that step-parent win through, states Ruth Webber.

Ruth Webber's most recent book, called *Split Ends: A Survival Guide for Stepchildren*,* shows how adolescents in particular can gain a sense of control over their own lives, in a merged family. This book, too, is positive, empathic, and written in a style that teen-agers understand. It will prove of great value if a parent or step-parent offers it to newcomers in the family. Of many pieces of advice that stood out for me, I believe parents would appreciate these:

> In stepfamilies, members need to be careful about the way they dress. It isn't really fair on other family members for you to go around in your jocks or undies. Because all family members are

not biologically related it can be disconcerting to step-parents or siblings to see you wandering around with practically nothing on. Likewise, you may feel uncomfortable about your step-parent or stepsiblings walking around practically naked. Don't put up with feeling uneasy. Voice your unease.

And this set of rules applies to fair fighting:
- Stick to the present (the past is not to be brought up).
- Listen to the other person without interruption.
- Stick to the topic.
- New issues cannot be introduced until the present one has been resolved.
- Always speak in a polite and conciliatory tone.
- Try not to make the other person feel guilty.

There is also wise counsel concerning sexual attractions within a stepfamily:

Being attracted to someone is normal. Keeping the lid on it is more difficult. A stepdaughter and stepfather may be physically attracted to each other. Both may be afraid of the emotion and try to avoid each other or be cold to each other as a way of coping. To act on the feeling would cause suffering to family members. If you are attracted to your step-parents or to a stepsibling, it may be helpful to talk it over with a counsellor who can help you deal with this difficult situation.

> Being attracted to someone is normal. Keeping the lid on it is more difficult. To act on the feeling would cause suffering to family members.

To partner or not to partner

Some people choose not to marry, living instead in de facto relationships or as 'singles'. While it would be unreasonable to suggest that only single people are lonely, there are nevertheless many organisations, small and large, to cater for the needs of lonely people. The special needs of grieving people are met through groups like Solace and Compassionate Friends. Funeral directors can put widows and widowers in touch with people in similar circumstances. Legacy Wives, Civilian Widows and pensioner groups are other supporting organisations.

Parents Without Partners is an international organisation providing a professional counselling service, with a strong back-up of volunteers. Many PWP branches have a twenty-four hour telephone counselling service. They support families and individuals through all kinds of crises, from separation and divorce to unemployment and parenting difficulties. Legal advice, emergency housing, social activities and children's programmes are all part of PWP's regular schedule. Its 'guidelines for lone parents', available through any PWP office, are sensible, practical and affirming. The JET Programme – jobs, education and training for sole parents – is run by Commonwealth government departments (Social Security, DEET and Human Services and Health) to help improve their lifestyle with increased income through employment.

John Stuart Mill, the English philosopher of 120 years ago, was an advocate of the marriage of two persons of cultivated faculties, between whom there exists:

> the best kind of equality, similarity of powers and capacities with reciprocal superiority in them, so that each can enjoy the luxury of looking up to the other and can have alternately the pleasure of leading and being led in the path of development.

As Mill said, this might be the dream of an enthusiast, but he maintained 'with the profoundest conviction' that this, and this only, was the ideal of marriage. Equality in rights and in cultivation was imperative. All opinions, customs and institutions that favoured any other notion were 'relics of primitive barbarism'.

Because of this, some very sane people choose not to marry or enter a permanent relationship. Recently the Reverend Kim Cruikshank wrote an article in her parish paper headed 'Single, white female'. This was the title of a film she did not see, but she used it for her article, because that is what she is. She has chosen not to marry for anything less than Mill's model. Here is part of what Kim wrote:

> I am a single, white female, much to the dismay of my mother, much to the disappointment of many friends, much to the desperation of others, but actually of little consequence to ME! Why is this so? Why are people so keen to see me married?

Some of the reasons she heard were that she would be looked after, would have someone to lean on, someone to stand with when opening the door to strangers, she would not be lonely, she was so good with children, and there would be 'someone there' for her. Kim was able to answer that she has all those things now; she has three meals a day, one day off a week, clean clothes, money coming in, a reliable car, many dear, close and supportive friends, her family, her cat and now a dog.

Kim wrote:

> As I understand it, no good model of marriage has one leaning on the other, but rather a mutual leaning. More like a lean-to, where one's leaning equals the other's, and so offers mutual support. I would never marry another, simply to lean on him – neither could I bear living with another who leant always on me ... And how many marriages do you know when the spouse is needed to open the door? Sounds a bit silly when we think about it, doesn't it?

Loneliness had little to do with the number of people who shared a house (or indeed a bed), she added, and she certainly enjoyed children very much, including her seven wonderful God-children, a few fabulous cousins, plus an assortment of friends' children whose lives were happily intertwined with hers.

> And when I think back to my own childhood, I remember many significant adults who taught me, inspired me, encouraged me, and who are dear to me still. Pity help any child who can only

look to his/her parents. And pity help any adult who is only concerned with their daughter's or son's welfare, and not for their community's children.

There are certainly many people 'there' for Reverend Kim. She knows who to call on in the middle of the night to get her to the doctor, she knows who to call on for a good cry, and she knows who will celebrate with her when she has good news. So, being 'Single, white female' is not so difficult, nor so unusual. In fact, she finds it can be great fun and just as rewarding, nourishing, sustaining and demanding as other ways of life.

> Throughout our parish, as indeed throughout the ages and throughout the Bible, men and women have lived as single people, either for a time or forever, and they give us no sense of somehow being incomplete, or waiting for something more. They, in their way, are quite alive and quite complete.

Even so, should she meet an equal who both stimulates and supports her, Kim is prepared to review her marital status.

The need for intimacy

As I began this chapter, a newspaper headline caught my eye: 'Sex and the elderly are still great bedfellows.' Not everyone would agree, but the experts assure us this can be, indeed should be, the case. Experience, time and communication are the keys to a good sexual life.

Professor Marita McCabe, Professor of Psychology at Deakin University since 1991, has spent twenty-four years in the area of sexual studies. She has conducted a study looking at the links between intimacy, sexuality and quality of life. Respondents were recruited from the electoral roll in order to make the study as representative of the general population as possible. Only one third of the replies came from men. Those men who did reply bared their souls, craving for, almost desperately willing to speak to someone who would listen. The study found that despite ninety per cent of respondents saying sex was important in relationships, sixty per cent had sex once a week, or less frequently.

One of the commonest problems among men is their failure to establish intimacy. Women on the other hand have a need for 'romance'. The combined elements of the male wish to be 'macho' and the female wish to be 'swept off her feet' can be very destructive indeed.

Professor McCabe thinks intimacy may be the key factor. 'Five or six years ago we were led to believe that every woman needed to experience orgasm, but these days it seems it is the intimate relationship, with or without orgasm, that matters most.'

The Sexual Behaviour Clinic* she conducts covers a wide spectrum of clients. Enjoying orgasm for women, enhancing sexual desire, increasing ejaculatory control, and dealing with erectile problems are topics for specific clienteles. The confidential treatment programme, set in professional private surroundings, usually requires from eight to ten visits on a fortnightly basis. There is no need for a medical referral, although it is helpful to pass on information about any tests or treatment from the doctor.

Disinterest in sex

Somewhat unexpectedly, Professor McCabe is finding that about half the men presenting to the Clinic express concern about their disinterest in sex. This 'sexual anorexia' is said to be one of the most difficult sexual disorders to treat. Inhibited sexual desire was formerly most common among women, especially among those women who had been raised to believe that sex was a wife's duty, rather than a pleasure in itself. These days she is seeing the numbers of women and men presenting with sexual problems more equally balanced.

Poor childhood experiences, low self-esteem, the stifling of sex in discussion, a strict religious upbringing and the lack of close friendships in adolescence can be factors relating to this problem for both men and women. Therapy can be helpful in such cases, if both partners are involved and both are willing to initiate sexual activity. Clients are encouraged to express their lack of arousal as a reality, without feeling guilty about it.

About one-third of Dr McCabe's male clients have erectile problems, and most of these can be corrected. 'Men at fifty are encouraged to accept that they are no longer twenty years of age', Dr McCabe stated. 'Rather than fighting the ageing process, they need to acknowledge their age, realise it will take longer to get an erection and that it will not be as rigid as it once was, but their performance can still be satisfactory for each partner.'

Another area of special study has been among women with secondary inorgasmia, that is inability to reach orgasm when at some stage previously they have been orgasmic. This can occur at any age, and may be related, for example, to body image, relationships or lifestyle. Issues relating to communication, conflict resolution, power and control are explored during therapy. The woman's inhibitions, performance anxiety and unwillingness to take responsibility for her own sexual pleasure are factors in the sexual interaction. At the same time the man's encouragement, respect and co-operation are required, together with the setting aside of the idea that his partner's orgasm is the proof of his own sexual adequacy.

If one of the partners is not interested in genital sex, Dr McCabe advises the matter can best be sorted out first by talking with each other. They then need to seek therapy, before it leads to major problems.

A fascinating supplement to the standard treatment programme offered in the Sexual Behaviour Clinic deals with sexual fantasy. Relaxation, visualisation, communication exercises, writing a fantasy diary, massage and aids such as videos and erotic literature may be used in this programme, depending upon the client's particular problem and his or her wishes. There are, as well, other supplementary programmes under the general title 'Exploring and Pleasuring the Sensual You'.

Many sex therapists advise couples not to try too hard, but to talk together in a relaxed way, *not* after heavy drinking, and *not* when they are anxious or tired. They can then discuss the possibility of new positions, in different places and at different times. Pelvic exercises are a positive way forward. Massage of the partner is also a pleasant, soothing means of 'togetherness', especially if time without interruption is set aside.

> Many sex therapists advise couples not to try too hard.

The right to sexual fulfilment

The importance of intimacy accords with the wider view held by Dr David Plummer, a specialist in sexual health. He believes the basis of mental health is the capacity to maintain intimacy. The chance to enjoy the intimacy of another person is one of the great opportunities of ageing, he states.

> The chance to enjoy the intimacy of another person is one of the great opportunities of ageing.

Addressing a national workshop on gerontological education, research and practice in 1993, Dr Plummer said this:

> Anybody who aspires to a fulfilling life would probably accept that that would include a right to sexual fulfilment. Yet a fulfilling sex life has probably been denied to many because our social processes often conspire to prevent that opportunity. Negative attitudes towards sexuality, or bad past experiences may poison the ability to relax and enjoy the pleasure of being with another person. Alternatively, outsiders may act to deny sexual opportunity in the belief that older people are asexual, or that sex should be only for procreation, or out of a sense that sex between older people is distasteful or amoral.
>
> Rather than assuming that people become sexless with advancing age, the constraint of pregnancy is removed, the pressure of children eases and the tiredness that comes from long

working hours is relieved. All of this provides a renewed opportunity to explore sexual feelings.

It should not be assumed that the physical changes of ageing reduce the opportunity to enjoy sex. It does seem to be true that many people experience a mellowing of sexual urges with increasing age, but providing people can shed the crude attitude that sex is about performance and intercourse rather than intimacy and pleasure, greater sexual fulfilment is likely.

The loss of a spouse is a heart-breaking blow, and one that can open a painful and lonely vacuum. But as time passes, the need to be alone and mourn will pass and be replaced with a need for company. Given sufficient time, that need may become sexual.

Ageing therefore provides an unexpected opportunity for romance, intimacy, pleasure and sexual fulfilment. Sometimes this may have to be recaptured, past attitudes may have to be unlearned and physical changes may require some adaptation. And of course, every modern sexually active older person should set a good example and be an expert on safe sex.

All of this is greatly appealing, but it is necessary to return to those who, in professional parlance, are 'sexually dysfunctional'. Not all of them are in the older age bracket, but many are. Professor McCabe believes it is not particularly helpful to use the notion of 'normality'. 'The frequency of desire, arousal, frequency of sex and orgasms, all these vary between individuals', she states. 'People can have unrealistic expectations of normality fostered by the mass media.' What is best for the individual couple in a relationship may be quite different from the media messages.

Menopause

In 1994 the Key Centre for Women's Health at the University of Melbourne had an American researcher, Professor Norma McCoy. She is interested in human sexuality and how hormones affect female sexuality during the menopausal transition.

Her most recent research project examined the effect of the birth control pill on women's sexuality. She looked at three groups of menopausal women – those not taking the pill, those taking monophasic pills (same amount of oestrogen and progestogen throughout the cycle) and those taking triphasic pills (varying amounts of oestrogen and progestogen during cycle).

A surprising result of Professor McCoy's research was that menopausal women using the triphasic pill had more sexual interest, thoughts and fantasies than women using no oral contraceptive. She did find, however, that women using oral contraceptives tended to have better relationships with their partners which may explain this finding.

In the area of sexual arousal, Professor McCoy found that menopausal women using the monophasic pill reported less vaginal lubrication than women using either triphasic pills or no oral contraception. This result may explain the lower level of arousal and enjoyment during sexual activity experienced by women using the monophasic pill. Norma McCoy believes that women using oral contraceptives may not be experiencing their sexuality to the fullest, and argues that research into oral contraceptives needs to take into account quality of life issues, such as sexuality, for women to be fully informed.

In short ...

1 Making a fresh start with a new partner provides an excellent opportunity for some professional counselling, regardless of age and experience. Why not grasp the opportunity to enhance your chances of success?

2 'New' marriages are catering more for individual needs and satisfaction. The key concepts are equity, role flexibility and negotiation.

3 Stepfamilies are like any other family: high points and low points, hard work and great rewards.

4 Mutual respect and courtesy between family members works wonders.

5 No marriage – or partnership – at all is better than one that is likely to fall short of expectations.

6 'Singles' are not necessarily lonely: there is more than one kind of loneliness.

7 Intimacy and good sex are not the exclusive preserves of the young.

8 Don't have unrealistic expectations – relax and enjoy what's possible.

9 Safe sex is still an issue, even for fifty-somethings the second time around.

11
Money matters – but how much?

Financial planning is a highly specialised activity. *Some* accountants and life agents have taken steps to acquire the necessary skills. *Some* stockbroking firms have created a financial planning section within their organisation. Stockbrokers and solicitors are not, in general, qualified to give the best advice on financial planning. Superannuation consultants act as advisers to boards of superannuation trustees, not to individuals, although some firms (like some stockbrokers) have developed a financial planning section.

> Financial planning is a highly specialised activity.

Financial advice

Financial advice, no matter the expert source, is seldom simple or easy to understand. Pension, superannuation and investment language is complex, and jargon is pervasive. In selecting an adviser, there are questions that must be answered. Ask yourself:

- How long has the adviser been in the industry?

- Does the adviser hold the required government licence?
- Is a report given to you in writing, and can you understand it?
- If not, will the adviser explain any parts that you do not understand, when you ask?
- Does the report give reasons why the investment is recommended for you?
- Does the adviser produce a regular newsletter, and is it easy to understand?
- What are the academic qualifications of the adviser?
- What research facility does the adviser use?
- Does the adviser provide ongoing review of your investments?
- Do you know any satisfied clients who use the adviser?
- Is the adviser a member of the Financial Planning Association of Australia?

Impartial financial advice has to be paid for. Two out of three Australian financial planners do not charge for the first interview, but this interview is only the beginning. The Australian Securities Commission advises planners to go slowly, to take time to get to know each client, and to make sure their needs can be matched in the best possible way.

> Impartial financial advice has to be paid for.

Even so, the initial interview with your adviser can be long, and the fee for this does not always take into account all the detailed work that is involved in preparing a written report. It is also unwise to choose an adviser solely on the basis of the lowest quote: better surely to have a relationship between client and adviser that is going to stand the test of time.

> It is unwise to choose an adviser solely on the basis of the lowest quote.

Investors often begin by asking questions such as: 'Where is the best place/fund/manager to invest my money?' As there is so much to be done before such questions can be answered, it would be much better to answer *after* the best strategy to follow is worked out, to suit that person's particular needs. *Where* to invest the money is the last stage of the overall plan.

So, back to square one, to the preparation of a budget, to establish how much the client needs, or would like to have to live on. We therefore begin with what sounds like an easy enough activity, budgeting, before going on to more complicated matters.

Budgeting in retirement

In private life budgeting tends to be seen as a chore. It is, however, the key to all financial planning, for it is simply an estimate of our income and our expenditure. It tends to be a means of restricting possibilities and choices. This is not the case, for with a little time and effort budgeting makes clear what we can do with our financial resources, and what we cannot. It means we can control our resources, and maximise them. Most importantly, there is the assurance that most of us are survivors, even of our poorest attempts at budgeting. The experience can thus help build up our confidence, and point to the limitations of our skill while helping us come to grips with our real financial situation.

Realistic forecasting about our future financial position, whether it be next week or next century, is what financial planning means. The key is to be flexible, realising that as our lifestyle and income change, so will our plan. Budget sheets, setting our sources of annual income on the one hand, and our annual expenditure on the other, are available from any financial institution or adviser.

An annual budget will show you the difference between your current income and your current cost of living. Hopefully, the former is the greater! If you have not kept records of paid bills and cheque butts over the previous year, you will need to itemise your spending over, say, the next three months, multiply the total by four, and add the annual items like car registration and insurance.

In budgeting your retirement expenditure, this should be based on current prices, for any attempt to allow for inflation at this stage would complicate the exercise. First you have to decide:

- Do I/we wish to maintain our current standard of living in retirement?
- Do I/we want to continue the same quality of food, clothing, holidays, and entertainment that I/we have now?

If the answers are yes, then that part of the estimate will be simple, since the current annual budget will serve as a base for our calculations.

We must also investigate ways to defer, reduce, or eliminate tax liability, and calculate the cost, tax-wise, of any decision we may make in this area. To repeat, there is much to be done before we reach that stage. Income splitting, for example, must also be considered as a way of reducing the overall tax liability for a couple in retirement.

At this point it is most important for the adviser to establish the client's 'risk profile', to ensure that clients will be comfortable with the types of products selected. Every good planner wants clients to sleep comfortably at night, without worrying about how their investments are performing.

The next stage is for the planner to prepare a written report with recommendations, and suggested alternatives. These should be explained to the prospective client, to ensure they fully understand the reason behind each recommendation, the risk (if any) involved, and the costs or fees applicable for each investment and the overall plan.

It can be a very time-consuming exercise to prepare such a report. The recommended investments must match the client's 'risk profile'. A comprehensive financial plan includes not only investment advice, but taxation, retirement, protection and estate planning issues. The report will also include cash flow (or income) projections, tax calculations, and, if applicable, pensions entitlements.

Finally, the paperwork is to co-ordinate and implement the plan, with provision for periodic reviews and plan updates.

In writing this chapter I took advice from Dr Kenneth Wright, Professor Emeritus of Accounting at the University of Melbourne (and long-term honorary treasurer of the former Early Planning for Retirement Association, now the Life Planning Foundation of Australia). His contribution to EPRA's Retirement Kit, under the heading of 'Finance', forms the basis of the following section.

In retirement, you will be living on money drawn from one or more of the following sources:

- pension from a superannuation fund
- income from the investment of a superannuation lump sum
- income from investment of other money saved or inherited
- earnings from part-time work
- Commonwealth age pension or service pension (full or partial)
- consumption of your capital.

Some people in retirement will be happy to live on an income substantially smaller than they have had during their working years. The need varies according to one's lifestyle, and to one's philosophy. If a small income is all that is required, perhaps the age pension with its fringe benefits will suffice.

> Some people in retirement will be happy to live on an income substantially smaller than they have had during their working years.

Government pensions are fluid; they are based on the cost of living wage, and they are taxable. People are often surprised to learn they may have an income of over $600 per week and remain entitled to receive a part-pension. The pensionable age for Australian men is sixty-five, for women it has been sixty but is progressively being raised to sixty-five. A wife need not have reached pensionable age for her sixty-five-year-old husband to claim a combined pension, but it will be only half the combined pension payable to a couple of pensionable age. Being the wife of such a person confers no pension entitlement, although she might be able to claim some other allowance from the Department of Social Security.

Once assessed as eligible, pensioners have the advantage of fringe benefits. These include discounts on electricity and gas, telephone and travel, municipal rates and many places of entertainment. Most State Governments now issue Seniors Cards that entitle holders to many concessions, both in public transport and in shopping of all kinds. Booklets listing the outlets where seniors may benefit show the huge range of possibilities for saving on purchases. Therefore even if your pension is small, it is well worth accepting, for these side-benefits add up. But you will do well to seek advice on how to get it.

> You should not scrimp during your working life and then find yourself with too much money at an age when your capacity to enjoy it may be reduced, and your priorities have changed or diminished.

If, however, your needs are more substantial, the age pension alone will not be adequate. Your income will depend on how much you have saved during your working life, how well you have invested this money and how you invested it at retirement. There are two phases in financial planning for retirement:

Phase 1: accumulation and investment of assets before your date of retirement.

Phase 2: re-arrangement or re-investment of assets at the time you retire.

How much you should save is a difficult question, and differs from person to person, from family to family. At one extreme, it does not make sense to maintain a high level of spending during your working life, only to have almost nothing left for your retirement. At the other extreme, you should not scrimp during your working life and then find yourself with too much money at an age when your capacity to enjoy it may be reduced, and your priorities have changed or diminished. Clearly, a balance is needed, and once again the preparation of a budget will help set out your current and future retirement needs.

Laurie Beckham, a financial adviser, reflecting upon a lifetime of business activity, has found that the happiest people in retirement are those with few or modest assets, and a full pension. The unhappiest are those on the borderline with just too many assets to qualify for the pension. They are worriers.

There are, however, certain changes that normally follow retirement. These questions must be answered:

- Will the mortgage be paid off?
- Will I/we save on home maintenance costs by doing them ourselves?
- Do older home appliances need replacing soon?
- Will the life insurance policies be converted to paid-up policies, with no further contributions required?
- Will travelling expenses be lower, with less regular commuting, and the opportunity to use age concessions on public transport?
- Will we be doing more interstate or overseas travel?
- Will more or less money be needed for clothing, entertainment and hobbies?

At this stage a financial adviser is most assuredly needed, if one has not already been used, to decide whether your existing savings, superannuation and any age pension entitlement will adequately cover the answers to the above questions.

Superannuation

And now to superannuation. If you belong to a superannuation fund that offers you a pension benefit defined as a percentage of your final salary and linked to the Consumer Price Index, this part of your financial planning will be relatively simple. Your retirement pension payment will relate to your salary and will include regular adjustments to allow for inflation.

But many superannuation schemes merely accumulate contributions and earnings, so that the size of the lump sum to be paid out on retirement will depend on the amount of future contributions and on the fund's future earning rate. If you belong to such a fund, you will have to estimate future contributions to the funds and its future earning rate. However, some superannuation funds will estimate your lump sum payment for you.

As you have estimated your retirement needs in terms of current prices, it is now necessary to estimate your lump sum entitlement on the same basis. In other words, the effects of future inflation must be excluded, so as far as future contributions are concerned, this is quite straightforward. They can simply be estimated as a percentage of your current salary. But it may not be simple to work out how the fund's earning rate has to be adjusted to remove the effects of inflation.

If you assume that your fund is earning eleven per cent yearly after tax, and that inflation is running at the rate of five per cent, then the purchasing power of your investment – or the quantity of goods and services it will buy – is growing at six per cent. In estimating the lump sum you will receive on retirement, you should, therefore, use a growth rate of six per cent, not eleven per cent, to make the result comparable with your estimated retirement needs.

Generally, the best investment for retirement income is a superannuation fund because of the tax advantages. Income from investment in such a fund is not part of your taxable income, though tax is currently paid by the fund at a rate not exceeding fifteen per cent. If you already belong to a superannuation fund

> Generally, the best investment for retirement income is a superannuation fund because of the tax advantages.

at your place of employment, you may be allowed to increase your contributions if your estimations tell you that you may have an income shortfall in retirement. Whether you belong to a superannuation fund or not, you can also buy superannuation from an insurance company or fund manager.

Before committing any substantial amount to additional superannuation, however, you should look at your reasonable benefit limit (RBL). Your adviser can help you with the necessary calculations.

If you need to save and invest more money for your retirement, your proposed contributions to another fund may lead to an eventual payout in excess of your RBL. This excess benefit amount would be taxed at the highest personal rate of tax, with no rebate allowance for the taxes already paid by the fund. Alternatively, you could convert the excess amount into an income stream, by rolling it over into an allocated pension or an annuity. The resulting income will be fully taxable at normal rates, with no rebate or allowance.

If you wish to put aside additional savings beyond your RBL, you could simply invest them yourself in debentures, property or shares. If you are in a high tax bracket, you would be better off buying bonds from an insurance company or friendly society. These bonds do not add to your taxable income unless ceased within ten years. Even then, tax rebates will apply.

If the rules of your superannuation fund provide for the payment of retirement pensions, and if you choose to take your entire benefit from the fund in pension form, there may be no need for any re-arrangement of your assets on retirement.

Usually, however, at least some part of superannuation benefits is paid in lump sum form at the time of retirement. At this stage, lump sum tax has to be paid unless the money is rolled over into an approved deposit fund (ADF), a deferred annuity fund (DA), another superannuation fund, an immediate annuity or an allocated pension. You can roll over into an ADF or DA only if you retire before the age of sixty-five, but only if you are gainfully

employed for at least ten hours per week. In that case, your money can be left in a superannuation fund until your employment ceases or until your seventieth birthday, whichever occurs first. Rolling over into an ADF, DA, or other superannuation fund confers two advantages:
- Payment on lump sum tax is deferred, and you can earn interest on the full amount, including the tax.
- ADFs and DAs enjoy the same favourable taxation treatment as superannuation funds.

If you have other sources of income or other savings that you can draw on for living expenses, it is usually better to use these other sources than to make withdrawals from a roll-over fund. However, in some circumstances, it is better to withdraw money from a roll-over fund, pay lump sum tax on it, and invest it elsewhere. In particular, this applies where your total superannuation benefit is close to, or has exceeded, your RBL.

Rolling over into an immediate annuity also avoids the payment of lump sum tax, and you can qualify for a tax concession that is more favourable than that granted to ADFs and DAs.

A further incentive to invest in an annuity is that a substantially higher RBL applies where at least half the superannuation benefit is used to purchase a complying annuity.

If you have turned sixty-five and you do not wish to put your money into an annuity, you can pay lump sum tax and be free to deal with your superannuation money as you wish. You may invest it to preserve your capital, you can simply spend it, or you can spend some and invest the remainder. If your spouse has a low taxable income, it may be possible to save some income tax by investing part of the lump sums in your spouse's name.

Another option open to you is that of taking an allocated pension. If you choose this course, you would roll over all or part of your lump sum into a superannuation fund which provides for the payment of allocated pensions. These pensions enjoy tax advantages similar to those associated with an immediate annuity; they do not, however, qualify you for a higher RBL.

After retirement

Managing your money in retirement is, of course, complicated by the fact that you do not know how long you — and your spouse, if you have one — are going to live. The three main ways of coping with this uncertainty are as follows:

1 Lifetime pension or annuity

Perhaps you belong to a superannuation fund that provides you with an indexed pension for life, together with a reduced pension for your surviving spouse. If not, it is possible to purchase an annuity that provides similar benefits.

Basically there are two types of annuities, but more than 101 variations, not all of which are offered by any one company. It is essential, therefore, to seek the services of an impartial adviser who can help you seek the best type of annuity to suit your own particular needs and circumstances.

> Managing your money in retirement is, of course, complicated by the fact that you do not know how long you are going to live.

One is commonly known as term certain, and can be taken out for a fixed term between one and up to twenty-five years. It is guaranteed to be paid whether you live or die (although at death it is usually commuted and a lump sum paid to your estate or beneficiaries).

The other is a lifetime annuity, and means exactly that. It will be paid as long as you and/or your partner keep living. Of course you can include guaranteed payment periods, and there are other options and guarantees that can be included.

Some are used as long-term or lifetime debentures, whilst others are more tax effective, and pension friendly, as part of the income is assessed as a return of capital and therefore not assessable as income by either the Tax Department nor Social Security.

If you believe that your expected needs in retirement will be modest, the Commonwealth age pension may play a large part in meeting those needs. The Department of Social Security also takes the view that part of each annuity payment that you receive from a lifetime annuity represents a return of capital. The Department therefore excludes that amount from the Income Test.

2 *Maintaining capital intact*
If can you live on the after-tax income from your investments, then your capital will remain intact. Some people like to keep their capital intact so that they can bequeath it to their children.

Both the dollar amount of your capital and its buying power need to be maintained to allow for inflation. If you invest in fixed-interest securities, such as finance company debentures, you may receive a comparatively large income, but inflation will cause the buying power of your capital, and, therefore, that of your income, to shrink each year. In other words, you would not really be maintaining your capital.

3 *Consuming your capital*
If you spend more than the income from your investments, you will have to eat into your capital. As the size of your capital shrinks, so will the income from it, so that each year you will be consuming more of your capital just to maintain your expenditure. Eventually, if you live long enough, your capital will run out, and you may have to rely solely on the age pension.

Consuming your capital is not necessarily unwise. You may well take the view that your income needs will reduce as you grow older, and that it is better to spend your money while you can enjoy it, rather than preserve it to buy a gold-plated wheelchair! You might decide, quite deliberately, that you would be prepared to manage on the age pension if you should live beyond a certain age. The important thing is that you should realise what you are doing, and the implications it can have on your future standard of living.

Housing matters
Our house is naturally of far greater import than its mere appearance. It is perhaps the greatest financial investment we ever make, and is an essential part of the fabric of our lives. It provides

not only shelter, but security and status. Brian Walsh, a Melbourne therapist who counsels many people troubled about moving, has a thoughtful phrase about the place we call home. He says every person's home is 'a warehouse of memories'.

It is important for older people, especially those who live on their own, to obtain council and other support services for maintenance tasks. These ensure the place not only looks well cared for, but also invites the owners to feel proud, happy, content, and supported in their home.

As we become older, children leave home and our own needs may be less in terms of space, both inside and outside the home. There are choices to be made about this most important issue. The key issue is 'Who makes the choice?' It should always be the home owner, usually the older couple or single person who sees the place of residence as that little bit of the world they call their own. Decisions about moving or staying should not be taken by adult children who think they know best. Loss of independence for any person usually leads to a loss of dignity. Clearly, the most harmonious decisions are made with the family in dialogue. Chapter 9, showing how families on farms are advised to proceed, with ageing parents having to make serious decisions about transition, is useful for every family facing this question.

> Decisions about moving or staying should not be taken by adult children who think they know best. Loss of independence for any person usually leads to a loss of dignity.

Where we live determines our access to services, support and care. A booklet on *Housing Choices*,* prepared by the Australian Council on the Ageing as a contribution to the bicentenary in 1988, gives practical advice, especially on 'staying put' or 'choosing to change'. As the booklet states, living at the right place at the right time in our lives can make a difference between leading a satisfying life, or a frustrating and lonely one. For older people, satisfactory housing is crucial to the quality of their lives.

Since World War Two there has been a rising rate of home ownership among older people. At the same time, governments have entered the field on three levels, in providing low-cost housing, in-home service and institutional care. South Australia led the way in the 1950s, by constructing 'cottage flats' for older people. Other states followed, providing bed-sitters and other forms of high density accommodation until it was realised that older people needed more than a place to sleep. Their need for a home was as strong as ever. Two- and three-bedroom units began to appear, with basic services like meals on wheels, home cleaning, gardening and maintenance, home nursing, podiatry and other services delivered by the community.

The 1980s saw the rise and rise of the retirement village, designed and built with the lifestyle of older people the priority. These vary greatly in terms of admission, cost, service and geographical location.

Staying at home among that 'warehouse of memories' needs serious consideration. Have you the physical, as well as the financial ability to cope for, say, the next ten years? Will you be able to manage the stairs? Is the garden going to prove a worry? Can you afford to pay a regular gardener? How much will the weatherboard house cost to paint? Is your house secure enough? How close are the shops, public transport, the doctor, the chemist and the church if you have to give up driving? For those in southern states, was that wonderful holiday in Queensland enough to persuade you to move there permanently? Did the warmer climate really cure those pains and aches?

All these questions, and more, only point to the importance of talking things over with spouse and/or children, and with a helpful financial adviser. All other options can be canvassed and visited. The many attractive retirement villages advertising their services can be checked out both by the Retirement Village

Associations operating in most states, and by Retirement Village Residents Associations. Make sure, however, you are prepared to move into less space, and be very close indeed to new neighbours of whom you have little or no knowledge. Some people find they need more, rather than less space in retirement, to spread about that new interest or activity. In any case, ask all kinds of questions if a retirement village beckons, especially about extra fees, community facilities, deduction for pensions and any other matter of concern.

The Abbeyfield Society, a not-for-profit British organisation established in Australia in 1981, has a lower profile but is worth considering. Abbeyfield's philosophy strikes a balance between independent living and serviced accommodation. It caters for people of limited means who prefer to live alone, but appreciate help, in this case in the form of a housekeeper who lives on the site and cooks two meals a day for residents in up to ten small units. Residents must come from their local community and the project is always built near familiar surroundings. Service clubs often initiate, and continue to support Abbeyfield.

For those with sufficient land on their existing property to consider dual occupancy, this is well worth considering – as long as one is prepared to live on half, or less than half the land one has tended for so long. One must also be prepared to accept the closeness of new neighbours.

Public housing is an option for people on low incomes, and some recent estates built by governments are very pleasant indeed. Waiting lists are usually the problem, but it is worth persisting with the public housing authority, or housing trust in your state or territory, if your income is within the acceptable range and this is to be your choice.

Leave a will, or leave a mess

At some stage along this financial path, preferably early on, it is crucial to make a will. Although so often overlooked and not discussed within even the closest of families, a will is one of the most important documents we are likely to sign. Tidying up this aspect of our personal affairs need not be a hassle. All one needs is careful planning, and some professional advice. A will is a formal declaration by which the person making it (called the testator) provides for the distribution of his or her assets and property (the estate) after death.

An estate typically comprises cash and deposits, real estate, shares and other securities, life assurance, business interests, and personal effects such as cars, furniture, jewellery. All debts, taxes and administration charges will be deducted before these assets are distributed.

To be valid, a will carries several requirements. It must be in writing, and signed by two witnesses who must declare they saw, together, the testator sign the document. The witnesses must not benefit from the will, nor be married to the testator. A person may change or revoke his or her will at any time.

There are many reasons for seeing that a will is made and placed in safe keeping, as early as possible. Most important, you and only you are in a position to decide how your property is to be distributed. Your family deserve that consideration. Making a will early enables you to choose an executor, obviously someone you trust and who will see to the distribution of your assets exactly according to the terms of your will. An executor may be a family member, and he or she may be a beneficiary, unlike those two witnesses to the will. On the other hand, the best help may come from an impartial outsider, like a solicitor or a public trustee. The commission such a professional charges may be well worthwhile.

The professionals will not only have the advantage of speaking with you personally to ascertain your precise wishes as the will is prepared, they will also be there, hopefully, to carry out your wishes after your death. Commonwealth and State death duties may have been abolished, but there are still areas on which you will need the advice of professionals, for example on capital gains. If a family member contests the will the advice of an impartial professional executor is obviously preferable.

If your will was correctly made in another country before you settled in Australia, it will be accepted in Australia. An existing will is automatically revoked by remarriage. If an unmarried person dies without a will, it does not go first to the immediate family, but to a de facto partner if there is one of two or more years' standing.

Wherever you lodge your will, your next of kin needs to be informed and the executor should be given a copy. It is good advice to leave a current inventory of your assets in the same place. One can buy blank will forms at any newsagent. They are straightforward and require no special knowledge of the law, nor the use of any legal language. Your own intention must be made concisely and clearly, that is all that is necessary.

A power of attorney is another matter to think about when making a will. The older one becomes, the more necessary this is, for sickness, accident or failing mental ability can limit one's ability to make decisions. By legally empowering another trusted person – or a trustee company – to represent us, we are ensuring that our wishes will be competently fulfilled. Again, professionals with current knowledge of the law are the best persons to act as power of attorney.

The sensible promotion during Senior Citizens Week by State Trustees in Victoria, and the Public Trustee in other states, alerted many people to the value of using an outside executor. At shopping centres they organised will-making sessions free of charge. During the year, they run a mobile service at suburban centres in the capital cities, as well as many regional centres. Pensioners, Seniors Card holders and people with Commonwealth health benefits can have their wills made on the spot, at discount prices.

The Australian Red Cross has prepared a free guide entitled *Caring for the Next Generation*,* which explains in simple language how to protect one's family and friends by making a will. It is obtainable through the Red Cross head office in each capital city. Even if a will has already been made, the booklet is a helpful check in ensuring that everything possible has been done to safeguard the future. Most Red Cross state offices will also provide a list of solicitors who will make or update a standard will for Red Cross supporters and their families, for a nominal fee. They must indicate that they have received a copy of the Red Cross wills booklet.

The will maker has of course no active part in the reading of the will – an event portrayed so often in film and literature. Advice is now emerging as to how offspring should talk to their parents about their expected inheritance. The advice usually runs like this: be tactful; don't anticipate death; ask about parents' goals and dreams for themselves and for you; discuss examples known in other families where distress or disappointment, or satisfaction and harmony, have followed the distribution of the estate.

The importance of maintaining good family relationships is usually in the parent's mind; it should also prevail among the potential beneficiaries. Another helpful entry to such conversations is the interests of the grandchildren. One adviser I know of adds this sensible warning: 'Expect nothing, and if something comes your way, it will be a nice surprise!' Most people will have heard or read the advertisements: 'Leave a will, not a problem'.

> If you die without making a legal will you have no control as to who will benefit from your estate.

You are said to die 'intestate' if you die without making a legal will. Trouble then arises. You have no control as to who will benefit from your estate. The court has to appoint someone to administer and distribute your estate in accordance with fixed legal rules, which may be quite contrary to what you would wish.

In extreme cases, in Victoria for example, if you leave no will and you have no next of kin, your assets could go into the state government's consolidated revenue account after a seven-year period. Making a will, even with the aid of a professional, does not cost a great deal. It is far, far less than the cost if your successors seek the court's interpretation of a home-made will.

A further argument in favour of making a will early, is that it is an appropriate place to express other wishes, in particular your wishes in regard to organ donation, and your funeral. We consider the funeral, that mysterious boundary between life and death, in the next chapter.

In short …

1 Financial planning has become increasingly difficult to manage, so much so that professional advice may be necessary in your case.

2 While you should be prepared to pay for this, be sure that you have chosen wisely and well.

3 Mind the jargon – don't be afraid to ask for things to be repeated if they are not clear, in terms you are familiar with.

4 In retirement, budgeting is essential, tiresome though it may be. It can help control your resources, and make the most of them.

5 Retirement may be the opportunity to simplify your lifestyle. This could be a matter of reviewing your philosophy of life, but could bring you new freedom.

6 Try to strike a balance between spending too freely while you are 'still young enough to enjoy it', and saving up for that gold-plated wheelchair.

7 Make your own decisions about whether you will stay put, or move to a different kind of accommodation.

8 Decide on where you will live while you are still fit, keeping in mind any possible future problems.

9 Making your will does not, in fact, speed up your day of departure, and postponing it does nothing more than leave a heap of trouble for your family. Again, do this while you feel full of life – and update it whenever circumstances change.

10 It is not taboo to discuss the will with the family, or for the family to approach the subject discreetly and tactfully with their parent/s.

12
Crossing the boundary of loss and grief

Grief and loss come in a myriad of ways. They are a natural part of human experience. We mourn the loss of a child, a lover, a spouse, a pet, the loss of a job, or of familiar surroundings. We grieve over an indiscretion, a broken friendship, a guilty secret, the indignity of defeat. Failing health can be terribly hard to bear.

> Grief and loss are a natural part of human experience.

A loved person falling into dementia can be tragic for a whole circle of family and friends. The farming family's loss of their life work is indescribably hard. The list goes on. Small griefs can tug at the heart as do large griefs. How to cope with the grief process, how to handle it better, usually demands time, along with the support and wise counsel of others.

From the first stages of shock, one is usually advised to keep busy, to stay near others who understand and who are available when needed for a talk, or a cry, or just a silent presence. It is important to express the emotion, no matter what that emotion is; anger, guilt, hostility, even panic are natural components of the grieving process. It is also natural to feel depressed, hurt or lonely, but the dark days will pass. If they do not, and distress shows itself in physical symptoms like headache, sleeplessness and continuing debility, it is wise to talk to one's doctor.

The struggle to adjust takes longer for some than for others. Life-shaping beliefs are called upon, and these are particularly significant at the time of death.

All this affirms the value of discussing, early on, what needs to be done when one member of a family dies or becomes incapacitated. The only time for rational discussion is when people are well, in their right minds and prepared to face the issues involved, especially the responsibility for others if one member must eventually be placed in a nursing home. The absolute imperative of preparing a will, as considered earlier, underlines the necessity for a shared knowledge and understanding of individual wishes. Advice given to farming families, about the importance of open and honest discussion, is just as vital for people wherever they live.

The value of funeral rites

It is important to understand that funerals are for the living, who need the chance to say goodbye. It is a rite of passage, as old as the human race, a unique point in every person's history, and therefore rightly called the universal experience. Funerals are shared events which celebrate the life of the one who has died, not the death itself. Family ties can be strengthened, beliefs about life and death can be restated, and the reality of the loss is expressed in tangible, sympathetic ways.

The Reverend Dr Charles Sherlock, editor of the national Anglican newspaper *Church Scene*, writes about the pastoral opportunities afforded by a funeral. He sees funeral rites as a community process, a personal event, and an act of worship.

From an anthropological perspective, a funeral can be seen as a community moving through stages in the process of grief. Whatever the particular relationships to the dead person of different individual people at the funeral, the rite enables the community *as a whole* to cross the boundary of loss. A funeral service is a 'ritual', a carefully shaped series of actions and words that assist a group to face a situation of danger, and cope with it ...

A key pastoral aspect of a funeral is the sense of completeness it can give. Ideally, those who participate are better able to close the book on the past, and begin to take up life once more without their friend. *It is thus important that the body leave those gathered, rather than those present leaving the body behind.* The sense of accompanying the dead person on their last earthly 'journey' is significant for all concerned. It is marked especially by care being taken in the way in which the body is received at, and leaves, the place where the funeral is to take place ...

> A key pastoral aspect of a funeral is the sense of completeness it can give.

Bereavement and health

A valuable book, *Bereavement and Health in Australia*,* was recently written by Dr Abe W. Ata. It provides a better understanding of grief among religious, ethnic, Anglo-Celtic and Aboriginal communities. It also aims to help carers by providing them with ways to view death more positively, to decrease death-related anxieties and encourage feelings of adjustment. He believes it has become absolutely necessary to introduce death education courses in high schools and tertiary institutions. Death not only visits the old, and besides, it is essential that preparation be part of life itself.

Dr Ata surveyed 300 people across eight cultural/religious groups from three areas, one urban, the other two country. Among his findings were:

- Affiliation to a religion can offer people great strength and sustenance when they deal with death, yet
- If religion has not been part of the routine life of a family, it can be a source of confusion.
- Surprisingly, the Anglo-Celtic cultures by and large continue to shun emotional expressions of bereavement as inappropriate, and somewhat distasteful despite their clinically attested value.
- The length of time of the grieving process was shortest among non-religious affiliates.
- Arab-born Muslims found their religious/cultural affiliation creating a better grieving condition than any other group.
- The large majority found funeral directors helpful and knowledgeable.
- Many reported a lack of awareness of grief counselling services.
- A large number believe in some form of life after death.
- A significant group reported some form of communication with the deceased.

The wisdom of planning a funeral

More and more people are realising the wisdom of *planning* a funeral, by seeking the advice of professionals. Funeral directors have become multi-skilled, for the industry is increasingly requiring training in mortuary work, in funeral management, and in bereavement. Three quarters of this country's funerals are carried out by members of the Australian Funeral Directors Association, who are bound to a strict code of ethics.

Most of us have contact with a funeral director only when a near relative or a close friend dies. An air of sombre mystery surrounds the industry, although its professionals are working hard at promoting themselves as thoughtful facilitators. Australia has been described as a death-denying society, for many of its citizens regard death as a taboo topic. Because death is so rarely discussed, its consequences are often not understood. Unresolved grief becomes an underlying cause of much emotional distress in people's lives. Some understanding helps us prepare for what is an inevitable eventuality.

Much valuable material is available through the Australian Funeral Directors Association (AFDA).* As part of its community service programme, one can obtain well-produced, easy-to-understand literature that would save much heartache if more people took the opportunity to use it. As the literature states, some understanding of what happens at the time of a death helps us prepare for its eventuality.

While this book is all about living life to the full, it still acknowledges that death comes, and it is wise to make even minimal preparation for it. This is of enormous help to the family. Clergy have told me that by far their greatest problems arise when a family does not know what kind of funeral arrangements the deceased would have preferred.

The doctor, who must provide a death certificate, is the first professional to be called. In religious families, the clergy are also contacted early, and they, with long experience, often take responsibility for making contact with an appropriate funeral director. If there is no religious tradition, location is a factor in making this choice, but the AFDA will always recommend a company that will provide professional understanding and caring service.

Initial interviews can be at home, or at the funeral director's offices. A myriad of alternatives are available, for funerals can be as different as the people they are for. Here are some of the decisions to be made:

- When and where will the funeral be held?
- What type of service is desired?
- Burial or cremation?
- Which coffin or casket, and clothing for the deceased?

- A viewing? (In South Australia it is mandatory for a family member to identify the body before cremation.)
- Who is to be involved?
- Who will be the pallbearers?
- What floral arrangements, motor vehicles, prayers, readings, music, and speakers will be appropriate?
- Will donations to an appropriate fund be suggested in lieu of floral tributes? If so, which fund?

It is not surprising that the Prices Surveillance Authority (PSA), when investigating the industry in 1992, expressed a good case for the pre-arranged, or a prepaid, funeral. The PSA stated that one advantage of planning, and paying ahead, was the opportunity to look around in one's own time for a competitive quote. There is, too, the knowledge that the bereaved family will be relieved of all such details at the time of their distress.

When the PSA published its consumer guide on the funeral industry, it made the point that a few people, for various reasons, may wish to make all arrangements for a funeral themselves. There is no legal requirement that a funeral director be used, and all the essential elements of a funeral can be legally undertaken by the relatives and/or friends of the deceased.

Some practical difficulties may be encountered, however, by anyone who attempts to bypass the services of a funeral director without prior enquiries. It is almost impossible, if starting at the time of death, to learn to do all that is required. The Redfern Legal Centre in New South Wales has published *Rest Assured*,* which addresses the difficulties of arranging a do-it-yourself funeral.

Less than five per cent of the funerals in Australia are of the 'essential care' type. This is restricted to transport of the body to the mortuary, a brief conference with the client, registering the death and obtaining the necessary certificates, transporting the body in a coffin to the crematorium or grave, committal with no ceremony, and has no provision for attendance of the bereaved at any point.

> It is almost impossible, if starting at the time of death, to learn to do all that is required.

It needs to be remembered that ashes following a cremation do not have to be collected and dealt with; this is always a decision for the family to make, in discussion with the funeral director.

In cities, the cost of a burial is usually significantly more than a similar funeral involving a cremation. In the country the difference is less, due to the reduced cost of land for burial sites. (*Through Deep Waters** is a resource book on loss and grief written especially for country families.)

A new phenomenon in the funeral industry has been the establishment of all-female companies. The first in Australia was established in South Australia in 1987 by Vanessa Hume. Her husband Keith Russell had successfully established Simplicity Funerals, and Vanessa, seeing the need for a woman's touch, created White Lady Funerals, now flourishing in all Australian states. It was thought to be the first all-woman funeral business in the world.

Judy Brain, the Melbourne manager of White Lady Funerals, explained that women have prepared the bodies of the deceased from time immemorial. Today, half of her clients are women, seeking a burial service for a male. These clients want to deal at this difficult time with another woman, and seek 'a woman's touch, with her gift for the finer details that come naturally'.

When there is no body, usually in the case of an aircraft or shipping accident, in time of war, or when the deceased has willed the body for scientific research, it is still important to acknowledge the death, and a memorial or thanksgiving service is a fitting ceremonial occasion to say goodbye.

Grief counselling

One of the more recent services introduced by funeral directors is that of grief counselling. As part of its community service programme, the AFDA has produced a series of sensitively written pamphlets.* These include such titles as 'What do I do when someone dies?'; 'What do we tell the children?' (a simple guide for adults to help children understand death); 'Creating Memories: when a baby has died'; and 'We need to say goodbye: why a funeral is important'.

Another AFDA pamphlet, 'It's all right to cry', is a survival guide for the bereaved. It sets out the stages in the grieving process, incorporating a number of physical, emotional and mental states, for they can happen in any order, and can leave the grieving person stuck in any one stage. There is usually a first reaction of shock and disbelief, then the emotional release, the loneliness of separation, maybe physical symptoms such as headache, backache, asthma or some other illness, pining, then relief that the deceased's pain and suffering has finally ended.

At some point there may be a sense of guilt, whether real or imagined, and depression. There may be anger towards the deceased, towards the medical team or towards God, inability to return to normal activities, and then light at the end of the tunnel. Life eventually becomes bearable again; one can rejoin the human race, recognising one's own capabilities and strengths, and having faith in others to help us cope.

> There is the need to feel support, to face reality, to express feelings and to re-establish one's self to go on living.

'It's all right to cry' sets out some of the most important needs of grieving people. There is the need to feel support, to face reality, to express feelings and to re-establish one's self to go on living. These needs can only be met by a caring listener who is aware, sensitive and patient.

Jan Tully works as an educator and counsellor in the area of grief and loss in both a private practice and with the Centre for Social Health established in Melbourne by the AFDA, which offers a certificate in bereavement studies for those whose work brings them in contact with grieving people. Jan is a civil funeral celebrant, who has officiated at over 600 funerals. The sudden, unexpected death of her husband gave her a new and entirely different experience of grief. He had observed his wife grieving with others, and because of his own anger at the way main-line churches acted as if they had a monopoly on rites of passage, he had requested that his own funeral be a civil one, with a simple graveside service. Jan reflected:

Honouring the wishes of someone you love is not always easy, for it often means doing something that would not be your own choice. After John's death I decided to stop working in the area of grief and loss, because I knew I would project my own feelings onto my clients.

In due course a couple of my friends who were facing death through AIDS-related illnesses asked me to help them plan their own funerals. Those with this virus really do plan ahead for the time they have left. It is far more than simply arranging for a prepaid funeral; they really think about what they want for this last ceremony, and whom they want to carry it out.

Jan now helps to train funeral directors, teachers, pastoral workers and others who face loss in their daily work lives.* She expresses great admiration for the ways in which they assist their grieving clients.

As a celebrant, and with her own experience as a mourner, Jan has reflected on the fact that the mourners are often still in a state of numbness and shock at the time of the funeral. They are not listening, no matter how comforting the words, the prayers, the music. It is, she feels, both a practical and thoughtful gesture to provide them with copies of what the celebrant and others have said, or even a tape of the whole service.

Part of Jan's work relates to understanding different cultural and social groups within the community, and their special practices and needs at their time of loss. She is particularly impressed with the Jewish Laws of Mourning and feels they offer not only practical and spiritual assistance, but are soundly based on the psychological needs of the bereaved. She feels that the Jewish acknowledgement of the various 'stages' or intensities of grief – particularly over the first year of mourning – are mirrored clearly in their Laws. This is more so, perhaps, than in the traditional Christian emphasis on resurrection and hope which, immediately after the loss, can actually seem an affront to the mourner's grief.

> Jewish tradition actively discourages any denial of the reality of death.

Jewish tradition actively discourages any denial of the reality of death. For that reason Jews find it helpful and practical to observe a fixed pattern of mourning. According to Orthodox tradition, burial must take place without delay; lengthy 'wakes' or lying in state for any length of time is foreign to Judaism. The sending of flowers is discouraged. Jewish tradition tries to keep funerals as simple as possible, because Judaism believes that all people are equal in death. This is demonstrated by the use of a simple wooden casket and the fact that the body is dressed in a simple white shroud. Many mourners have found the act of pouring a shovelful of earth onto the casket, once it is lowered into the ground, to be therapeutic; it helps to accept the totality of their loss. Cremation is not common, for this is seen as a contradiction of the biblical prophecy 'Dust returneth unto dust'.

After the funeral service, the first period of mourning is called Shiva, which literally means seven, for the seven days of mourning to follow. 'Sitting Shiva' is observed by the family and close friends, who come to console the mourners, in the form of prayer services, and by a demonstrably quiet presence. A neighbour considers it an honour to bring the first meal after the burial service, and this comes preferably in a wicker basket, again to prevent any sign of competition.

> A neighbour considers it an honour to bring the first meal after the burial service.

Shiva is followed by progressively longer and less intense stages of mourning, but throughout the mourning period, the Kaddish prayer is recited daily. The Kaddish is an Aramaic prayer more than 2000 years old; it says nothing specific about death — its theme is the greatness of God.

Jewish law mandates a full year of mourning only for one's parents. The mourning period for other relatives, including spouses, terminates at the end of *shloshim*. *Shloshim* is the period of thirty days after burial, with lesser restrictions as the mourners begin to continue with their lives. Whatever the period, mourners are discouraged from participating in public celebrations, such as weddings.

Unique funeral link

A world first is claimed by the Australian company, John Allison/Monkhouse, in establishing Funeral Link.* This is a service that allows mourners to participate in a funeral service from anywhere in the world, as long as they have access to a telephone. Distant mourners are not only able to hear the service; they may also address the people attending the service.

The first Funeral Link service occurred when an Australian family had relatives and friends in Canada and the United Kingdom who were unable to return for the service. All parties agreed to participate in the funeral via the telephone. A second service, linking families in Sri Lanka and Australia, established this innovation as helpful to all concerned. Funeral Link is now most commonly used by mourners throughout Australia. These people may be bed-ridden, unable to travel, or have other commitments such as work or child care preventing their attendance. Funeral Link is also used in nursing homes, hospitals and retirement villages.

Other innovative services offered are the Creative Funeral Group, the Mock Funeral, and the Widows and Widowers Groups. Each has a specific function. In the Creative Funeral group, people come together to discuss how they would like to arrange last rites, especially as they would differ from normal traditional practice. 'They are anxious to discover if what may be a way-out idea is acceptable, and possible', managing director Clive Allison explained. 'One person wished to know if it would be possible to have the ashes of a deceased person mixed with clay and made into a vase. Another wanted to know if it would be all right to have balloons at the ceremony.' The answer in both cases was yes.

The Mock Funeral was recommended by a psychiatrist who was seeing many patients seriously unable to come to terms with their loss. The body of the deceased was usually not available for burial, so a final goodbye had not been possible. In the Mock Funeral, held in the psychiatrist's rooms, a coffin is used with the name of the deceased inscribed, and a dignified ceremony is carried out, to help the grieving person accept the reality of the death.

In short ...

1 Death is not the only cause of grief and sense of loss. Do not deny yourself the need to grieve over any loss that is significant for you.

2 Seek professional help if the grieving process causes physical distress, and seems to be lasting too long.

3 As in making a will, and planning your future housing options, it is useful to plan your funeral while you are fit and well. This can also save your family some problems and keep you in control of affairs.

4 Funerals do not have to be grand occasions. A modest, simple funeral can have as much dignity and significance as an elaborate one.

5 If you choose to arrange your own funeral, you have time on your side to enable you to investigate the possibility of bypassing the funeral industry. But consult the family first.

13
Tomorrow is opportunity waiting

Now that we have dealt with the basic issues – the soundness of our health, housing and financial position – we can engage the future with a sense of purpose and integration.

Dr Terence Seedsman is Associate Professor Gerontology at Victoria University, and has the gift of speaking in lay person's language when addressing a lay audience. All his work has been dedicated to what he calls 'the forward journey'.

A deliciously exciting age

Terence Seedsman rightly sees the true potential of ageing as 'a deliciously exciting challenge'. We must throw out all negative images about retirement. We must abandon all thoughts of withdrawal, isolation, seclusion, departure, debilitation, quarantine, and boredom. They *will* go if we have a healthy level of self-esteem! Think about the positives:

> We must throw out all negative images about retirement, all thoughts of withdrawal, isolation, seclusion, departure, debilitation, quarantine, and boredom.

- opportunity
- freedom
- alertness
- relaxation
- openness
- curiosity
- enjoyment
- fun
- patience
- leisure
- learning.

Can you think of other positive words? There should be no wrinkles on the brain!

As Seedsman states, in the end it is a matter of balancing the negatives and positives that are part and parcel of our everyday lives. We not only accept our former life as meaningful, whatever the ups and downs that entailed, but also look to a future with enthusiasm and optimism, even though the future will also have its ups and downs. A healthy life will always involve elements of doubt, despair, optimism, curiosity and wonder.

A mind stretched in search of self

So we come back to learning. Learning is called a therapeutic tool for older people. It gives them a sense of power by overcoming feelings of helplessness. Learners feel more capable, discover goals and purposes, and find fresh roles. Learners are regarded more positively, and they react to others more positively. And they learn more about themselves.

Seedsman writes of the exhilaration of a mind stretched in search of self. 'A mind wasted at any age is a personal and national tragedy.' Failure to take the necessary action to lead a full and meaningful life is perhaps the greatest tragedy of all. Seedsman's book, *Ageing is Negotiable*,* has an opening message: 'To be

> To be meaningful, life ought always to be work in progress.

meaningful, life ought always to be work in progress. Anything else is a form of voluntary retrenchment from a labour of the utmost importance'.

None of us knows precisely what route our future will take, nor what will best satisfy us. We have to taste a variety of offerings, explore one further, or perhaps pursue a number. There is no magic recipe to guarantee a full and worthwhile life. Only *we* can say in which direction our enthusiasms are pointing. As Edward de Bono states, in happiness, as in cooking, there is a brew of ingredients to suit different tastes.

Seedsman sees retirement as something akin to relocation in a new country. It means change, but change that opens up new horizons.

The role of peacemaker

In later years, there is, importantly, another role to play. It is that of peacemaker. All persons can claim to be peacemakers, if they so wish. It begins in the home, moves into the community and then, perhaps, into the wider, fragmented aspects of society. The only place to begin is where we are.

> All persons can claim to be peacemakers. It begins in the home, moves into the community and then into the wider, fragmented aspects of society. The only place to begin is where we are.

Compassion, availability, and a listening ear are the qualifications needed in reconciliation. Of course it costs time, comfort, personal plans, and sometimes sleep. I heard an address on this topic, and the speaker warned: 'If you want to be a bridge, you have to be prepared to be walked over'.

Most Australians in their third age have already adapted remarkably well to change. They have seen their country emerging as an independent nation comprising many cultures, they have seen the motor car provide endless mobility, and the contraceptive pill lead to a dramatic sexual revolution. Most have spent fewer hours at work than their parents, suffered economic recessions, experienced the immediacy of worldwide news, seen wars and bushfires explode on their television screen, and wondered at the intricacies of technology. No-one in all of human history has seen life change so fast.

There is life still to be lived, nevertheless, and older people are freer to choose the pace. So, whatever your choices as you move into and past middle age, go for them! The passionate pursuit of life itself is the true goal. Loris Wilmot, a key speaker at Life Planning seminars, has this to say to the fifty-somethings:

> You have a responsibility to the next generation. You can demonstrate that life has been, and is, worthwhile. You have values to uphold, values of proven worth. You are a model for the next generation. We don't want question marks to close our lives, but more and more answers!

In short ...

1 Look at ageing as a challenge.

2 Think of your future life as a work in progress.

3 Accept the past as meaningful.

4 Learn! It gives you power.

5 Change opens up new horizons – don't fear it or reject it – use it.

6 Be a role model for the next generation.

Useful resources

Chapter 1   Early planning

* *Books and literature*

Don't Kiss Your Money Goodbye: How to Choose a Financial Planner. Free from Financial Planning Association of Australia, 50 Queen Street, Melbourne 3000. Freecall 1800 337 301.

* *Other resources*

Life Planning Foundation of Australia, 341 Queen Street, Melbourne 3000. Produces a retirement kit, updated regularly.

Chapter 2   Humanising the workplace

Morgan and Banks (head office), Grosvenor Place, 225 George Street, Sydney 2000. Offices in Parramatta, Canberra, Melbourne, Adelaide, Brisbane and Perth.
Outplacement consultants, placing people made redundant.

Chapter 3   Transition – to what?

* *Books and literature*

Sheehy, Gail, *Passages*, Bantam, New York, 1977.
―――― *Pathfinders*, Bantam, New York, 1982.

Chapter 4 Leisure and recreation

Department of Arts, Sport and Tourism, all states. Includes Department of Sport and Recreation. Recreation programmes for seniors.

Embroiderers Guild has offices in Sydney, Melbourne, Brisbane, Adelaide and Perth, and in many regional centres such as Launceston and Newcastle.

School for Seniors runs programmes for small, friendly groups in many Tasmanian centres. Contact adult education officers through the Department of Tourism, Sport and Recreation, Trafalgar Building, Collins Street, Hobart 7000.

Chapter 5 Contributing to a thinking society

✻ *Books and literature*

Expectations of Life: Increasing Options for the Twenty-first Century, Report by House of Representatives Standing Committee for Long Term Strategies, AGPS, Canberra, 1992.

Laslett, Dr Peter, *A Fresh Map of Life: The Emergence of the Third Age*, Weidenfeld and Nicolson, London, 1989.

Seedsman, Dr Terence, *Ageing is Negotiable*, Employ Working Effectively, PO Box 275, St Kilda 3182, 1994.

✻ *Other resources*

Australian College for Seniors, University of Wollongong, Northfields Avenue, Wollongong 2522.

Australian Volunteers Abroad, Overseas Service Bureau, 71 Argyle Street, Fitzroy 3065. Offices in other capital cities.

Council of Adult Education, 256 Flinders Street, Melbourne 3000.

Open Learning Australia, Locked Bag 60, Alexandria 2015 and GPO Box 1188, Melbourne 3001.

U3A Network Victoria Inc., CAE Centre, 256 Flinders Street, Melbourne 3001.

Chapter 6 Are you keeping well?

* *Books and literature*

Chiarelli, Pauline, *Women's Waterworks: Curing Incontinence*, Gore and Osment Publishing, Sydney, 1990.

Cooking for One or Two, Home Economics Association and Council for the Ageing (Victoria), 126 Wellington Parade, East Melbourne 3002.

How to Relax and Reduce Stress, NSW Health Department.

Millard, Richard, *Bladder Control: A Simple Self Help Guide*, 2nd edn, MacLennan and Petty, Sydney, 1996.

Morawetz, Dr David, *Sleep Better Without Drugs*. Book and three audio tapes, 18 Mangarra Road, Canterbury 3126. Freecall 1800 066 044.

Neild Gilmore, Louise, *The Carers Handbook – How to be a Successful Carer and Look after Yourself, Too*, Allen & Unwin, Sydney, 1995.

Now's the Time to Stop: Help for Older Smokers, QUIT. Tel. 13 1848.

Pinnock, C. B. (ed.), *Simply Busting: A Guide to Better Bladder and Bowel Control*, Wakefield Press, Adelaide, 1993.

Ryles, Judy, *Microwave Cooking for Kids*, Five Mile Press, Melbourne, 1995. Simple recipes for seven- to seventy-year-olds.

* *Other resources*

'Active at Any Age', a project of Heart Foundation and Vicfit (part of Department of Sport and Recreation, Victoria), 123 Lonsdale Street, Melbourne 3000.

Alzheimer's Association. Freecall 1800 639 331.

Australian Nutrition Foundation, 260 Kooyong Road, Caulfield 3162.

Carers Association of Australia (national office), PO Box 3717, Weston 2611. Freecall 1800 817 7746. Offices in every capital city.

Continence Foundation of Australia provides information through GPO Box 9919 in your capital city. Books on continence problems available through Continence Foundation of Australia, 59 Victoria Parade, Collingwood 3066.

Heart Foundation of Australia (national office), PO Box 2, Woden 2606, and has offices in every capital city and in Newcastle, Cairns, Gold Coast, Rockhampton, Toowoomba and Townsville.

Chapter 7   Health and gender difference

* *Books and literature*

Farrell, Elizabeth and Westmore, Ann, *The HRT Handbook*, Anne O'Donovan Pty Ltd, Melbourne, 1993.

The Key to Women's Health. Quarterly magazine of the Key Centre for Women's Health in Society (see below).

* *Other resources*

Gutbusters (head office), 40 Miller Street, North Sydney 2060.

The Key Centre for Women's Health, 209 Grattan Street, Carlton 3053.

Prostate Info-Line. Toll-free tel. 1800 066 889.

Chapter 8   Beating the statistics

* *Books and literature*

Breast Cancer in Australia. Free booklet from your state cancer organisation. Freecall 13 1120.

Condon, Loraine, *A New Way of Life*, HarperCollins, Melbourne, 1995.

Living and Loving. An American booklet showing how people with arthritis can enjoy a satisfactory sex life. Available from Arthritis Foundation Victoria, PO Box 130, Caulfield South 3162.

What are the Options? (prostate cancer), National Health and Medical Research Council.

* *Other resources*

For a free mammogram at an accredited assessment centre, tel. 13 2050.

Australian Cancer Society Inc. is the national federation of independent state and territory cancer organisations based in capital cities. Contact 15 Theodore Street, Curtin 2605. Copies of the leaflet 'Non-cancerous enlargement of the prostate' available from the Publications Officer, NHMRC, GPO Box 9849, Canberra 2601.

Arthritis Foundation (national office), Suite 902A, Kingersley House, 33 Bligh Street, Sydney 2000. Offices in every capital city.

Diabetes Australia (national office), 5/7 Phipps Place, Deakin 2600. Offices in every capital city.

Chapter 9 Planning the future down on the farm
* *Books and literature*

Bush Voices. Newsletter of WA rural network for women. Contact Lorna Morrisey, Noongall Station, Yalgoo 6635.

The Buzz. Newsletter of Australian Women in Agriculture. Contact Sharon O'Brien, Yarrawonga 3730.

The Country Voice. Newsletter of Queensland Women in Agriculture Inc. President Jan Darlington, 'Three Moon', Monto 4630.

The Country Web. Newsletter of Rural Women's Network, NSW. Contact NSW Agriculture, Locked Bag 1, Orange 2800.

Network. Newsletter of Rural Women's Network, Victoria. Contact RWN State Government Offices, corner Mair and Doveton Streets, Ballarat 3250.

'Retirement and Estate Planning for Rural Families', paper. Yanco College, NSW.

The Rural Book. The Commonwealth Government's information access service for country people. Information on social security, finding a job, assistance for farmers, soil and tree projects, landcare, and so on. Free and post-free to country people, GPO Box 858, Canberra 2601.

Scutt, Jocelynne A. (ed.), *City Women, Country Women: Crossing the Boundaries*, Artemis, Melbourne, 1995.

Transferring the Family Farm: What You Can Do, Department of Agriculture, 1991.

McGuckian, Nigel, Stephens, Mike, Brown, Robert and McGowan, Helen, *Your Farm, Their Future – Together*, University of Western Sydney, Hawkesbury.

'The Transfer of the Family Farm Business in a Changing Rural Society', (final report), edited by Dennis Gamble et al. for Rural Industries Research and Development Corporation, 1995.

* *Other resources*

Country Care Link, Rural Women's Network NSW. Confidential information and referral service for NSW. Contact NSW Agriculture, Locked Bag 1, Orange 2800.

Country Women's Association has state headquarters in every capital city.

Countrylink, Commonwealth Government access service. Toll-free tel. 1800 026 222.

'Handing on the Family Farm: Let's Get Started'. Kit available from Family Farm Consulting, PO Box 1174, Crows Nest 2065.

Let's Talk. Communication for farm families. Thirty-minute video. CB Alexander Agricultural College, Tocal, Paterson 2421. Toll-free tel. 1800 025 520.

Foundation for Australian Agricultural Women, National Secretariat, GPO Box 1634M, Melbourne 3001.

Chapter 10   Repartnering in the nineties
* *Books and literature*

Noller, P. and Callan, V., *Marriage and the Family*, Methuen, Melbourne, 1987.

Webber, Ruth, *Living in a Stepfamily*, ACER, Melbourne, 1989.

—— *Split Ends: A Survival Guide for Stepchildren*, ACER, Melbourne, 1996.

* *Other resources*

Anglican Marriage Education and Counselling Service is the name of the organisation in Victoria. Anglican agencies use different names in different states; for example, Anglican Community Services in South Australia, and Anglican Family Care in Queensland.

Centacare – Catholic Marriage Education Programme (all states).

Relationships Australia Inc. (formerly Marriage Guidance) has state offices in every capital city.

Sexual Behaviour Clinic, Deakin University, Burwood and Toorak campuses, Victoria. No medical referral required.

See also Key Centre for Women's Health, Chapter 7.

Chapter 11   Money matters

Caring for the Next Generation. Free guide to protecting family and friends by making a will. Red Cross, head office in each capital city.

Housing Choices. Booklet from Australian Council on the Ageing
See also Chapter 1.

Chapter 12   Crossing the boundary of loss and grief
* *Books and literature*

Ata, Dr Abe W., *Bereavement and Health in Australia*, David Lovell Publishing, Melbourne, 1994.

Grief and Loss, the Pain of Caring. Free to carers from Carers Association in each state.

Rest Assured: A Legal Guide to Wills, Estates and Funerals, Redfern Legal Centre, NSW.

Pamphlets on death, dying and grieving from the Australian Funeral Directors Association (see below).

Through Deep Waters. Challenge of Change Programme, 1994. Continuing Education Office, CB Alexander Agricultural College, Paterson 2421.

❋ *Other resources*

Australian Funeral Directors Association (national office), 700 High Street, Kew East 3102. Offices in every capital city.

Funeral Link, John Allison/Monkhouse (head office), 45 Glenvale Crescent, Mulgrave 3170. Freecall 1800 638 637.

General

Friedan, Betty, *The Fountain of Age*, Vintage, London, 1994.

Scutt, Jocelynne A. (ed.), *Glorious Age: Growing Old Gloriously*, Artemis, Melbourne, 1993.

Council on the Ageing Australia, 464 St Kilda Road, Melbourne 3004.